Teaching Brass
A Resource Manual

by

Wayne Bailey
Arizona State University

Patrick Miles
University of Wisconsin-Stevens Point

Alan Siebert
College Conservatory of Music
University of Cincinnati

William Stanley
University of Colorado

Thomas Stein
University of Missouri-Kansas City

Boston   Burr Ridge, IL   Dubuque, IA   Madison, WI   New York   San Francisco   St. Louis
Bangkok   Bogotá   Caracas   Kuala Lumpur   Lisbon   London   Madrid   Mexico City
Milan   Montreal   New Delhi   Santiago   Seoul   Singapore   Sydney   Taipei   Toronto

Higher Education

TEACHING BRASS: A RESOURCE MANUAL
Published by McGraw-Hill, a business unit of The McGraw-Hill Companies, Inc., 1221 Avenue of the Americas, New York, NY, 10020. Copyright © 2008, 1992 by The McGraw-Hill Companies, Inc. All rights reserved. No part of this publication may be reproduced or distributed in any form or by any means, or stored in a database or retrieval system, without the prior written consent of The McGraw-Hill Companies, Inc., including, but not limited to, in any network or other electronic storage or transmission, or broadcast for distance learning.
Some ancillaries, including electronic and print components, may not be available to customers outside the United States.

This book is printed on acid-free paper.

1 2 3 4 5 6 7 8 9 0 QPD/QPD 0 9 8 7 6

ISBN: 978-0-07-352658-4
MHID: 0-07-352658-4

Vice President and Editor-in-Chief:
   Emily Barrosse
Publisher and Sponsoring Editor:
   Christopher Freitag
Associate Development Editor:
   Beth S. Ebenstein
Editorial Assistant: *Marley Magaziner*
Executive Marketing Manager: *Sharon Loeb*
Managing Editor: *Jean Dal Porto*

Project Manager: *Margaret H. Leslie*
Art Director: *Jeanne Schreiber*
Designer: *Marianna Kinigakis*
Photo Research Coordinator:
   Natalia C. Peschiera
Production Supervisor: *Jason I. Huls*
Composition: *11/13 New Caledonia,*
   Thompson Type
Printing: *40# Alt Book 690, Quebecor World*

Library of Congress Cataloging-in-Publication Data

Teaching brass: a resource manual / by Wayne Bailey . . . [et al.]. — 2nd ed.
   p. cm.
  Includes bibliographical references (p.), discography, and index.
  Co-authors: Patrick Miles, Alan Siebert, William Stanley, and Thomas Stein.
  ISBN-13: 978-0-07-352658-4 (spiral : alk. paper)
  ISBN-10: 0-07-352658-4 (spiral : alk. paper) 1. Brass instruments—Instruction and study.
I. Bailey, Wayne, 1955– II. Miles, Patrick John. III. Siebert, Alan. IV. Stanley, William James, 1954– V. Stein, Thomas G.
  MT418.T4 2008
  788.9071—dc22

2006012948

The Internet addresses listed in the text were accurate at the time of publication. The inclusion of a Web site does not indicate an endorsement by the authors or McGraw-Hill, and McGraw-Hill does not guarantee the accuracy of the information presented at these sites.

www.mhhe.com

CONTENTS

Teaching Brass: A Resource Manual is designed as a college textbook for brass methods students and as a resource manual for school music teachers. As a class text, it can be used in courses that cover one to four instruments, either separately or simultaneously, in programs varying in length from four to sixteen weeks. As a resource manual, it can be used when working with beginning to advanced students.

Teaching Brass features in-depth coverage of each brass instrument by a specialist on that instrument. It provides more specific information on instruments, equipment, embouchures, articulations, and special techniques than is available in any other single source. The chapters offer instruction about how to play brass instruments, with an emphasis on diagnosing and solving common problems. Included for reference are harmonic series and fingering charts that teach the use of alternative fingerings, warm-up exercises and practice routines, and instrument-specific information on what types or brands of equipment to use in particular settings. By using this text, the teacher of the brass methods course can use one book to teach both brass performance and brass pedagogy.

In addition to information on playing and teaching brass instruments, this book offers a unique series of technical exercises specifically designed for college students. The exercises are presented in four-part score form. They progress on the basis of the harmonic series of the instruments, focus on specific technical problems typically encountered by beginning brass players, and are designed to increase in difficulty at a rate compatible with college-aged students' learning abilities. The authors believe that presenting new notes as they occur in the chromatic series is the fastest method of teaching fingerings and slide positions to college-aged students. This presents new notes in a different order than would normally be used in a beginning method book for use with school-aged children; the authors do not recommend presenting new notes in such a system with younger beginners who lack musical experience.

The exercise schedule is based upon a course that meets for a total of 2½ hours per week. The instructor can use the book as a guide to student technical development in courses that teach four, two, or a single instrument in 4, 8, 10, or 16 weeks. The full-score design allows the text to be used in single- or mixed-instrument courses. Throughout the text the reader is referred to specific exercises that address specific points in the reading. This is intended to guide the reader in use of the exercises.

The instrument-specific chapters are aimed at providing an excellent overview of the instrument while providing the teacher with some specific information. The authors present a text for the teaching and learning of the instruments at the beginning level. The suggestions for breath control, embouchure, and articulation are made to create the foundations and fundamental concepts of playing. As such, performance techniques used by advanced brass players in specific settings such as jazz, marching band, or orchestral playing are beyond the scope of the book.

The authors wish to express gratitude to the following individuals and companies whose efforts have contributed greatly to this text: Larry Morris, of Kolacny Music Company of Denver, Colorado, for providing the instruments and equipment for the photographs; Yamaha Corporation of America; and Chris Knighton, Brian Winkelbauer, Mark Sandusky, and Doug Prunk for serving as models for the photographs.

Wayne Bailey
Patrick Miles
Alan Siebert
William Stanley
Thomas Stein

INTRODUCTION

Teaching Brass: A Resource Manual can be used both as a textbook for a college course and as a resource manual for the music educator.

If you are a student using the book in a class, you should read all of the introductory chapters (that is, "Acoustics of the Brass Instruments," "Breath Control," "The Embouchure," "Articulation," and "Brass Instrument Equipment") before reading the chapters on specific instruments. These introductory chapters give an overview of the concepts common to all brass instruments and make the information in the chapters on the instruments (Chapters 6 through 10) easier to understand. For example, you should gain a general understanding of how to form a brass embouchure from Chapter 3, "The Embouchure," and add to this the specific information in Chapter 6, "The Trumpet," to understand the trumpet embouchure.

The music student in a college course of this type is quickly overwhelmed by the performance demands and amount of information required to teach the brasses. We suggest that you concentrate your efforts in two areas: personal performance of the instruments and problem solving. When you work with your own students, you must be able to quickly diagnose and solve problems of embouchure, holding the instrument, and breath control. It is this information that we think you should learn and retain. Other information, such as suggested equipment, literature, fingerings, and care and maintenance, can be found by referring to this book when needed. We also believe very strongly that you should concentrate on your own performance on the brasses. You will have performance problems similar to those of the younger students that you will soon teach. By experiencing and overcoming these problems, you will become a better teacher.

The teacher in the field can use the book as a guide to solving specific problems. Each of the chapters on the individual instruments covers embouchure problems and their solutions, specific equipment suggestions, warm-up and practice routines, special and advanced technique instruction, and literature lists. These topic areas can be located quickly through the Table of Contents.

The exercises in the back of the book are intended to be used in the college course and are designed to be more time-efficient than exercises found in traditional beginning methods books. These exercises are very different from exercises written for the young beginner in that they progress rapidly and assume knowledge of notation. The exercises also differ in that **they progress down the harmonic series rather than in diatonic scale patterns.** This system was adopted to better teach the seven-position or seven-combination fingering system used on the brasses.

The authors are brass players and teachers who, combined, have more than 130 years of experience in public schools and universities. All have taught brass methods courses at a variety of colleges/universities, and three (Bailey, Stanley, and Stein) developed brass methods courses and this textbook while colleagues at the University of Colorado. Their combined teaching experience encompasses the nation—from Connecticut to California, Texas to Minnesota. Together, they have taught brass classes in 19 states and 25 institutions.

Wayne Bailey is Director of the School of Music and Professor of Music at Arizona State University. Prior to his appointment at ASU, he held similar positions at the University of Tennessee in Knoxville and at Texas Tech University. A trumpeter and band director he has also served on faculties at East Tennessee State University; the University of Colorado, where he was also Assistant Dean; Hastings College; Alabama State University; and the Howell, Michigan Public Schools. Dr. Bailey holds a Bachelor of Music Education degree from Iowa State University, a Master of Music in trumpet performance from the University of Michigan, and a Doctorate of Musical Arts in instrumental conducting from the University of Colorado. Dr. Bailey is the author of three widely used music education textbooks: *Aural Skills for Conductors, Teaching Brass: A Resource Manual,* and *Complete Marching Band Resource Manual,* as well as a number of band and brass arrangements and music education journal articles. A well-respected music administrator, Dr. Bailey has been Chairman of the Committee on Ethics for the National Association of Schools of Music (NASM). He is currently a member of the national Commission on Accreditation and serves as an external evaluator of music programs for NASM.

Patrick Miles is Professor of Horn and Director of Orchestral Activities at the University of Wisconsin-Stevens Point. As a hornist, he has performed with a number of orchestras which include the Green Bay Symphony, La Crosse Symphony, Fox Valley Symphony, Central Wisconsin Symphony, Pamiro Opera Company, Des Moines Symphony, Eugene Symphony, Eugene Opera Company, Oregon Coast Music Festival, Flagstaff Festival of the Arts Symphony, Arizona Opera Company, Quad-Cities Symphony, Cedar Rapids Symphony, Cedar Falls-Waterloo Symphony and the Joffrey Ballet. Prior to his appointment at UWSP, Dr. Miles taught at Iowa State University, Oregon State University, and Grinnell College. Dr. Miles received his Bachelor of Music degree from Northern Arizona University and his graduate degrees from the University of Iowa, where he studied with Paul Anderson.

Alan Siebert is Associate Professor of Trumpet at the College Conservatory of Music, University of Cincinnati. A former member of the San Diego Symphony Orchestra and principal trumpet in both the San Diego Opera and San Diego Chamber Orchestras, Mr. Siebert has performed and recorded with

Summit Brass and taught at the Keystone Brass Institute. He was principal trumpet with the American Sinfonietta, the resident orchestra for the Bellingham Music Festival. *Hornpipes*, his solo album, was released on Integra. He has recorded with Pro Arte, Integra, New World, Discovery, Klavier, and Summit Records. He is on the board of directors for the International Trumpet Guild, and he is a member of the Carillon Brass and the Dayton Philharmonic Orchestra. Professor Siebert has also taught in the public schools of Connecticut and at the University of Minnesota-Duluth.

William Stanley is Associate Professor of Trombone at the University of Colorado. Prior to his appointment, he performed as a member of the Grammy award-winning Chestnut Brass Company. He performs in the Boulder Brass, the Colorado Ballet Orchestra (principal), the Central City Opera Orchestra, and as substitute/extra with the Colorado Symphony. He has presented master classes and clinics for many organizations and schools, including the International Trombone Association, Music Teachers National Association, and the Colorado Music Educator's Association, and hosted the 1998 International Trombone Festival at CU. He has authored articles and reviews for the *International Trombone Association*. He has taught at Temple, Eastern Illinois, and Millikin Universities. He performs in a wide variety of musical settings, and has frequently performed and recorded on historical brass instruments. He holds a BME degree from the University of Kansas and MM and DMA degrees from the University of Illinois.

Thomas G. Stein is Associate Professor of Tuba and Euphonium at The University of Missouri-Kansas City. A native of Michigan, he received the Bachelor of Music (with high distinction) and the Master of Music degrees in Tuba Performance from the University of Michigan, Ann Arbor. Prior to coming to Missouri, Stein taught at Central Michigan University, The University of Colorado at Boulder, and The University of Southern Mississippi. He has performed with numerous orchestras, wind ensembles, and chamber ensembles: Mississippi Symphony, principal tuba; Colorado Mahler Festival Orchestra, principal tuba; Colorado Festival Orchestra; Aspen Festival and Chamber Orchestras; Detroit Symphony; American Tuba Euphonium Quartet; Twisted Steel Quartet; Missouri Brass Quintet; Capital Brass; and the Colorado Brass Quintet. Mr. Stein is very active throughout the United States as a recitalist, clinician, soloist, and has been a guest artist in residence at several universities and academies. As a soloist/artist he has appeared with several orchestras and wind ensembles throughout the United States, has been featured in a variety of state, regional, and national/international conferences, and has appeared in six European countries. Mr. Stein's students are very active and successful in state, regional, national, and international competitions. Recently, his students have won numerous awards in major competitions: International Tuba-Euphonium Solo and Quartet Competitions; Falcone Solo Euphonium Competition (Artist Division); International Women's Brass Conference Solo Competition; Colonial Euphonium-Tuba Institute Solo Euphonium Competition; National Music Teachers Association State, Regional and National Collegiate Artist Solo Competitions; National Association of College Wind and Percussion Instructors National Solo Competition; Great Plains Regional Tuba Euphonium Conference Solo Competition; Texas Regional Tuba-Euphonium Conference Solo Competition; and the Southeast Regional Tuba-Euphonium Conference Solo and Quartet Competitions.

Acoustics of the Brass Instruments

The acoustics of brass instruments have been the source of considerable conjecture, testing, and study. When reviewing the results of formal tests, one is often confronted with various charts or graphs or a baffling array of formuli filled with seemingly meaningless numbers. While this might be productive reading for some, it is unlikely that the music teacher in front of a beginning band class would ever need so much technical information in order to be effective. This chapter describes in lay terms the physics of brass instruments and is intended to provide an overview of the workings of brass instruments.

Brass instruments are "lip-reed" instruments; that is, the vibrating sound source is the lips of the player held in such a manner as to make a steady tone or frequency. A column of air blown through the lips is the energy source that initiates and sustains the vibration. When the vibrating lips are placed in a cup or cone-shaped mouthpiece at the end of a brass instrument, a tone can resonate, as described in the next paragraphs.

The Overtone Series

With some experimentation the beginning brass player soon finds out that, without engaging any valves or moving the slide (with the instrument in its open position), many different pitches can be produced. This is a result of what is termed the "overtone series." A generic brass instrument of a given length has the potential to resonate certain predictable pitches in the constant interval pattern shown in Figure 1–1. This overtone series is of such importance in the playing and teaching of brass instruments that the music teacher should become very familiar with this constant interval pattern.

When any one of the pitches of the series is presented in the mouthpiece by vibrating the lips at the correct frequency, that pitch will be resonated (amplified) by the instrument. The basics for manipulation of the lips and breath to create the correct "buzz" will be discussed in the chapter on each specific instrument.

Figure 1–1   The Overtone Series

The lowest pitch of the overtone series is referred to as the "fundamental." The pitches above it are called "partials," or "overtones." For the sake of consistency, this book will refer to the pitches above the fundamental as partials.

Each of the brass instruments has a unique overtone series that is determined by the length of the instrument in its open position. See the chapters on the instruments, Chapters 6 through 10, for these specific overtone series.

It becomes obvious that there are a limited number of notes available when an instrument is in the open position. To obtain more notes, extra tubing is added to the instrument. This creates a longer air column inside the instrument and, consequently, a lower pitch. When the second valve is depressed, extra tubing is added so that a new overtone series is available on the pitch exactly one half-step lower than that of the open instrument (the trombone moves the slide out to second position to create the new overtone series). The first valve (the third position, on trombone) adds enough tubing for the tone yet another half-step lower and the resultant overtone series. This process continues through what is called the "chromatic fingering pattern"—open, 2, 1,1–2, 2–3, 1–3, 1–2–3 (corresponding on the trombone to positions 1 through 7). Each successive fingering adds tubing to increase the overall length of the instrument so that complete chromatic capability is achieved. The chapters on specific instruments in this book each contain a chromatic fingering chart based on the overtone series.

Intonation Tendencies of Brass Instruments

Brass instruments, because of the laws of acoustics, have inherent intonation problems. It is necessary for the music teacher to be aware of these intonation tendencies and to know how to compensate for them.

The overtone series is out of tune when compared with the equally tempered scale. Among the first eight partials, the fundamental and the second, fourth, and eighth partials are generally in tune. The third and sixth partials are slightly sharp, the fifth is slightly flat, and the seventh is so flat that it is generally unusable.

As valves are engaged or, on the trombone, the slide is moved, these same intonation tendencies persist as each new overtone series is created. As valves are used in combination, certain distinctive intonation tendencies occur. To make a given length of tubing produce a pitch one half-step lower, approximately 6 percent of the original length must be added. A generic instrument of 100 inches becomes 106 inches (the open instrument plus the tubing opened by the second valve). To make that 106-inch instrument sound a half-step lower, 6 percent of *its* length must be added (6.36 inches added by the first valve). The instrument is now 112.36 inches. To lower it another half-step, the second valve is normally added in combination with the first valve (see the chromatic fingering pattern that was described in the previous section). However, 6 percent of 112.36 inches is 6.75 inches. Adding the second valve will add only 6 inches to the instrument. What the second valve adds is 0.75 inch too short, making the 1–2 valve combination slightly sharp. This same tendency continues through the chromatic fingering pattern as set lengths of valve tubing are added in combination to meet ever-increasing length requirements. Specific techniques used to cope with this problem are listed in the chapters on the different instruments.

Temperature also affects the intonation of brass instruments. When a brass instrument is cold, it will sound flat; when warm, it will be sharp. The cause of this is most often thought to be the varying speed of the air moving through the instrument. Imagine the compounded difficulty facing a young brass player, playing a note in a flat partial using a sharp fingering in cold weather. Teachers must become familiar with the intonation tendencies of the brass instruments and the unique techniques used by each instrument to cope with them.

Selected Bibliography

Aebi, Dr. Willi. *The Horn and Its Inner Acoustics,* Chicago: Schilke, n.d.

Backus, John. *The Acoustical Foundations of Music,* New York: Norton, 1969.

Benade, Arthur. *Horns, Strings and Harmony,* Garden City, N.Y.: Doubleday, 1960.

Earlge, John. *Music, Sound, Technology,* 2nd edition, New York, Van Nostrand Reinhold, 1995.

Fletcher, Neville and Thomas Rossing. *The Physics of Musical Instruments,* New York: Springer-Verlag, 1990.

Kent, Earl L. *The Inside Story of Brass Instruments,* Elkhart, Ind.: C. G. Conn, 1956.

Moravcsik, Michael J. *Musical Sound: An Introduction to the Physics of Music,* New York: Paragon House, 1987.

Schilke, Reynold O. *Schilke Brass Clinic: The Physics of Inner Brass and of Effects of Various Materials and Their Treatment,* Chicago: Schilke Music Products, n.d.

C H A P T E R

Breath Control

Producing a satisfactory tone on any brass instrument depends in great measure on the proper use and control of the breath. The exhalation of air across a properly formed embouchure causes the lips to vibrate. This vibration is the basis of the brass tone and is greatly affected by both the speed and the steadiness of the column of air. To produce and sustain any pitch or phrase, the student must learn proper breathing methods; at rest (meaning regular, or day-to-day, breathing) inhalation and exhalation will not produce the desired tone on any of the brasses. Even though the student is relearning to breathe, this new method of breathing must still be as relaxed and natural as possible.

The Diaphragm

To diagnose and solve breath-control problems, brass teachers should be familiar with parts of the body that affect the breathing process. The diaphragm (Figure 2–1) is a large, dome-shaped muscle and membrane structure that separates the abdominal and chest cavities. During inhalation, the diaphragm contracts downward and flattens out, allowing the chest cavity to expand vertically. This contraction of the diaphragm allows the lungs to expand and take in air. The diaphragm actually relaxes during exhalation, returning to its dome shape and reducing the volume of the chest cavity.

The Thorax

The human chest cavity is also capable of horizontal expansion through enlargement of the rib cage, or thorax. The thorax is controlled by a group of connected muscles called the "intercostal" muscles, which, when contracted, cause the thorax to expand in area. The diaphragm and the intercostal muscles are connected, thus creating a simultaneous vertical and horizontal expansion when all

Figure 2–1   The Diaphragm

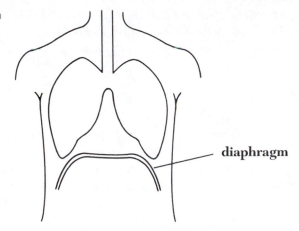

diaphragm

are contracted. Because of this, the "work" portion of breathing is accomplished during inhalation. These muscles relax during proper exhalation.

Points of Resistance

During inhalation, the air column should not meet with any points of resistance. However, the column of air may meet with at least three major resistance points during exhalation: the glottis, the tongue, and the aperture.

The Glottis

The glottis is actually not a "thing"; it is a "space." It is the space created by the opening and closing of the vocal cords and is often a first point of resistance during exhalation. The size of the opening changes greatly during normal activities such as talking, coughing, or sighing. Most brass teachers advocate using a very open glottis during brass playing, thus creating very little resistance to the air column at this point.

The Tongue

The tongue is the second point of possible resistance to both inhalation and exhalation. By placing the tip of the tongue and the back of the tongue in various positions in the mouth, one can create degrees of resistance to the air column, varying from no resistance to total resistance. Each of the brasses uses the tongue differently as outlined in the instrument-specific chapters.

The Aperture

The aperture produces the final (and for some brass instruments the only) physical resistance point to the air column during exhalation. The aperture, also a space, is created by the air column as it blows a hole in the embouchure during exhalation. The size of this hole is regulated by the degree of tension of the lips and the volume and speed of the air column.

Proper control of these three resistance points is different on each of the five major brass instruments and is essential for good tone production.

Posture

Developing good posture is essential to proper breathing techniques. If a brass player slouches while sitting or standing, or if he or she places the body in a rigid position, the lungs, diaphragm, and intercostal system cannot function.

When sitting, the student should sit forward with the back away from the chair, the feet flat on the floor, and the spine in an upright, noncurvilinear position. In assuming this position, the student must be careful not to raise the chest too high or allow any muscles to become rigid.

When standing, the student should avoid slouching or tensing the chest and abdominal areas. Twisting or contracting of the chest and abdominal areas reduces the air capacity of the lungs.

Inhalation

The process of breathing involves two motions: inhalation and exhalation. The player should always inhale through the mouth. The glottis must be very open and the tongue down and out of the way so that the incoming air encounters no resistance. The inhalation should be a very rapid intake of a large quantity of air. The simultaneous contraction of the diaphragm and intercostal muscles allows for a "deep" breath that fills the lungs. When inhaling, the player should feel as if the lungs are filled from the bottom first, then upward.

When discussing a topic as abstract as proper breathing, you may find analogies useful. For example, to achieve the proper vertical and horizontal expansion, students may be asked to "feel" that they are growing taller. (Students should not raise their shoulders during this exercise.) To provide the incoming air column with no resistance points, students might imagine the glottis and oral cavity to be large enough to swallow an orange or a baseball. Proper inhalation might feel like a rapid, silent gasp of air or a deep yawn. To visualize deep breathing, students could compare inhalation to filling a glass, from the bottom to the top. Any analogy used should evoke thoughts of relaxation and openness of air passages.

Exhalation

The air should not be held in the lungs after inhalation; exhalation should begin immediately. Exhalation for the brass player is not the "normal," passive expelling of air. The air should be projected into the instrument in a steady column to produce an unwavering tone. The player does this by relaxing the diaphragm and intercostal muscles in a smooth, controlled motion while expelling the air from the lungs. This controlled relaxation of the diaphragm may be accomplished by contracting the abdominal muscles around the waist.

The speed with which the air column is released helps regulate the volume of tone and the speed of vibration of the lips.

A useful exercise to improve the exhalation process is to ask the student to hold his or her hand at arm's length in front of the mouth. The student, if projecting the air properly, will be able to feel a strong air blast striking the hand when the air is blown through the embouchure.

Common Problems of Breath Control

When learning to play brass instruments, students encounter several common problems. Most of these problems involve the inhalation process. The single most common breathing problem is clavicular breathing. This is very shallow, upper-chest breathing; you can often spot it if you see a student's chest or shoulders rise during inhalation. To correct the problem, you might use some of the analogies suggested earlier in this chapter.

Retention of "stale" air can often lead to tension in the chest and abdominal muscles or even to hyperventilation. Most common on the high brasses, stale air occurs when the player does not expel all of the air in the lungs before taking another breath. Encourage the student to take fewer and larger breaths to correct this problem.

Another common high-brass problem is "setting" the breath. This is caused by holding the breath in for a short period of time before beginning to exhale. The inhalation-exhalation process involves a smooth turnaround of the air column. The breath should not stop between inhalation and exhalation. This problem is often identified by explosive attacks and overblown pitches.

Air columns that move too slowly are also very common. Usually caused by tension in the throat or abdominal muscles, or by tongue resistance, this problem is often called "squeezing" the tone. The tone produced is an unsupported, weak sound, and the player should be encouraged to relax the throat and abdominal muscles, place the tongue on the bottom of the mouth, and release the air column faster.

Breathing Exercises

Specific exercises to develop breath control while playing are included in Chapters 6 through 10. However, brass players will also benefit from breathing exercises that can be done away from the instrument. Here are some suggestions:

To Improve Inhalation

1. Slow inhalation exercise:
   a. Place the hands on the sides of the waist in order to feel the horizontal expansion achieved in correct inhalation.
   b. Slowly inhale, filling the lungs. The student should feel the stomach area expand, first from the bottom and then upward to the chest cavity.
   c. Exhale in a rapid "sigh" with no resistance points.
2. Rapid inhalation exercise: Repeat exercise 1 with rapid inhalation.

To Improve Inhalation and Exhalation

1. Inhale for eight counts at a speed equivalent to a metronome setting of 100. Exhale through the embouchure (with no lip vibration) for a duration of sixteen counts. Repeat, decreasing the duration of exhalation by two counts until exhalation reaches the point of eight counts.
2. Repeat exercise 1 with the duration of inhalation equal to six, four, and two counts, and finally one count.

The brass student should recognize that the correct inhalation-exhalation process is not "normal" breathing, but it is "natural." A new breathing method is not needed; simply learning to enhance the natural breathing method to expand the lung capacity will suffice to achieve proper breath control. You may find it most effective to provide the student with a correct model to imitate rather than focus the student's attention on the specifics of breathing.

Selected Bibliography

Berv, Harry. *A Creative Approach to the French Horn*, Harry Berv; 1977.

Brown, Merrill. *Teaching the Successful High School Brass Section*, Park, 1981.

Bush, Irving. *Artistic Trumpet Technique and Study*, Hollywood, CA: Highlands Music, 1962.

Conable, Barbara. *The Structures and Movement of Breathing*. Chicago: GIA Publications, 2000.

Farkas, Philip. *The Art of Brass Playing*, Rochester, NY: Wind Music, Inc., 1962.

Gregory, Robin. *The Trombone: The Instrument and Its Music*, London: Faber & Faber, 1973.

Kelly, Kevin. "The Dynamics of Breathing," *The Instrumentalist*, December 1983, pp. 6–12.

Kleinhammer, Edward. *The Art of Trombone Playing*, Evanston, Ill.: Summy-Birchard, 1963.

Pilafian, Sam and Patrick Sheridan. *The Breathing Gym*, Focus on Excellence, Ft. Wayne, IN, 2003.

Province, Martin. "Marching Band Warm-Ups for Stiff Chops," *The Instrumentalist*, August 1988 (reprinted as a part of "Marching Band Rehearsal Techniques," August 1997).

Weisberg, Arthur. *The Art of Wind Playing*, Schirmer, 1975.

Editors. *Selected Breathing Masterclasses*, Windplayer Publications, Malibu, CA, 2002.

Zi, Nancy. *The Art of Breathing*, Barton Books, 1986.

3

The Embouchure

How the Embouchure Functions

The term "embouchure" refers to the way in which one's oral cavity, lips, and facial muscles are used when playing a musical instrument. On brass instruments, this involves an airstream passing over the lips to cause them to vibrate against each other. This vibration, or "buzz," is then transmitted into the mouthpiece and amplified by the instrument to produce a tone. The faster the vibration, the higher the buzz or tone. The speed of the vibration is determined by the tension and pucker of the lips and the amount and speed of the air column.

The tension of the lips is regulated by the muscles surrounding the lips and in the jaw and cheeks. The proper interaction of these muscles creates a sort of tug-of-war in which there should not be a winner. The idea is to allow the muscles surrounding the mouth (the orbicularis oris muscle) to control the amount of pucker used in the embouchure and the cheek and jaw muscles to control the corners of the mouth. The authors do not believe it is necessary for the brass student to know the names of the facial muscles. However, if further information is desired, you should consult Philip Farkas's book, *The Art of Brass Playing*. You should refer to Chapter 2, "Breath Control," in *this* book for information regarding the air column.

In order to play a brass instrument, it is essential to develop the strength of these sets of muscles. This development (or endurance) is usually taught through the use of long-tone and lip-slur exercises. Included in each of the chapters on the instruments are exercises that develop the embouchure (see the sections on warm-up and practice routines).

Forming the Embouchure

The authors strongly believe that the embouchure on each brass instrument must be formed differently. Included in the instrument chapters are pictures of "correct" embouchures and information on how to form them. However, all brasses share some common embouchure traits. The following six items should be considered for all brass embouchures:

1. The oral cavity (the inside of the mouth and throat) must be open and relaxed, with the tongue on the bottom of the mouth.
2. The jaw should be lowered and firm. It should be flat or pointed, depending upon the facial configurations; and the upper and lower teeth must be approximately aligned.
3. The aperture (the opening in the lips created by the expulsion of the air column) should be oval in shape. This shape should occur naturally with the proper balance of pucker and firmness in the corners of the mouth.
4. The lips should be together, but not pressed together. The corners of the lips should be firm and in a "frowning" position.
5. The mouthpiece must be placed correctly on the lips. The chapters on the instruments contain specific instructions concerning mouthpiece placement.
6. The lips should be moist to aid in flexibility.

Each of the chapters on the instruments contains more specific information on embouchure formation and how each instrument differs from these general concepts.

Common Embouchure Problems

The brass teacher must be able to quickly diagnose and solve embouchure problems. Use of a mouthpiece visualizer (see Figure 3–1) is highly recommended to aid the teacher in identifying problems. These problems differ, as do their solutions, from instrument to instrument. The authors believe that the

Figure 3–1   Mouthpiece Visualizer

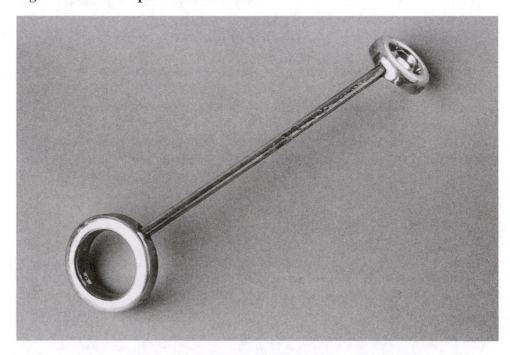

following are the most common embouchure problems encountered on all of the brasses:

1. The "smile" embouchure (see Figure 3–2). This embouchure problem is easily detected by looking at the corners of the mouth. It is produced when the corners of the mouth pull up as the student tenses the lips rather than pull downward in a frown position. This problem usually causes lack of upper range, flexibility, and endurance, and a tone that is sharp. The student should be encouraged to frown to tense the muscles and to "grip" the outside rim of the mouthpiece with the lips.

Figure 3–2
Smile Embouchure

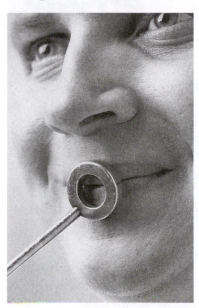

2. The "bunched-up" chin (see Figure 3–3). Most common on horn, this problem creates a flat, tubby tone quality and a lack of low range and flexibility. It is often caused by a clenching of the jaw or by a rolling or bunching of the bottom lip, or by both. To fix the problem, the player should point or firm the chin and relax the lower lip.

Figure 3–3
Bunched-up Chin

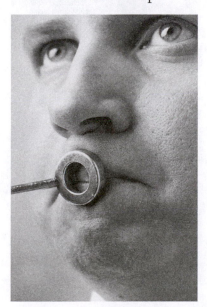

3. Playing with the mouthpiece too low (see Figure 3–4). This is common to all the brasses and creates endurance, range, and flexibility problems. The chapters on specific instruments discuss the proper placement of the mouthpiece for each instrument.

Figure 3–4
Mouthpiece Too Low

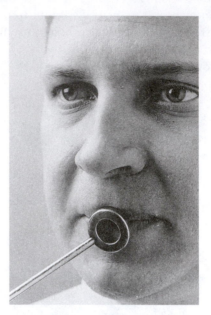

4. Playing with the mouthpiece not centered over the aperture. This problem can easily be diagnosed with the use of a mouthpiece visualizer. The player with this problem usually has a stuffy, sharp sound and a limited range.
5. "Puffed-out" cheeks (see Figure 3–5). Most common on the low brasses, this problem is created by weak embouchure muscles. Accuracy and endurance problems are usually evident, as well as an inability to play softly or with a normal articulation. The player with this problem must strengthen the embouchure muscles and direct the airstream toward the mouthpiece.

Figure 3–5
Puffed-out Cheeks

6. Excessive pucker (see Figure 3–6). This problem is easy to detect visually and causes a tubby sound with a limited range. The player should relax the orbicularis oris muscle and firm the corners to a frown position.

Figure 3–6
Excessive Pucker

7. Excessive mouthpiece pressure. Probably the most common of all embouchure problems, this occurs when the player allows the rim of the mouthpiece (rather than the corners of the mouth) to hold the lips in position to create a buzz. This problem is often the cause of severe endurance and flexibility problems and a limited upper register. The player should strengthen the corners of the mouth and review the holding position of the instrument to correct this problem.

It is important to remember that there is no "generic" brass instrument embouchure. You should carefully study the chapters on specific instruments to gain further information on embouchure techniques and problems of the individual instruments.

Selected Bibliography

Berv, Harry. *A Creative Approach to the French Horn*, Harry Berv, 1977.

Farkas, Philip. *The Art of Brass Playing*, Rochester, NY: Wind Music, Inc., 1962.

———. *A Photographic Study of 40 Virtuoso Horn Players' Embouchures*, Atlanta, Georgia, Wind Music Inc., 1970.

Kleinhammer, Edward. *The Art of Trombone Playing*, Evanston, Ill.: Summy-Birchard, 1963.

Weast, Robert. *Keys to Natural Performance for Brass Players*, Des Moines, Iowa: The Brass World, 1979.

Articulation

The function of articulation on any brass instrument is to assist the initial forward motion of the airstream and to provide different sounds at the beginnings of notes as dictated by various musical notations. Three types of articulations are possible: slurring between notes, tonguing at the beginning of each note, and beginning a pitch without the tongue. The third method is not recommended on the brasses because it produces an unclear beginning to the pitch and cannot be depended on to produce a pitch at a specific time.

Several types of slurs and tonguings are used on the brasses. The brass player must be able to produce smooth lip slurs (slurring between two pitches without moving valves or slide positions) and precise single, double, and triple tonguing. (Double and triple tonguing, also referred to as "multiple tonguing," are explained in each of the chapters on specific instruments.)

Tonguing Basics

The tongue is used to interrupt, not stop, the airstream. To produce as fast a tonguing stroke as possible, only the tip of the tongue should be used. The player should move the tip of the tongue in an up-and-down motion, *never* an in-and-out movement. The tongue should remain relaxed and should return to the lower part of the mouth after the tongue stroke. The student brass player might think of the attack as a pulling away of the tongue from a point on the roof of the mouth.

Brass players use different tongue syllables across the range of the instrument to produce varying sounds. Generally, the syllables progress from "ah" in the low register to "ooh" in the middle register and to "ee" in the upper register. Brass players start these syllables with either a *d* or a *t,* depending upon the musical notation. The *d* syllable (combined with "ah," "ooh," or "ee") produces a softer articulation than does the *t* syllable and is often used for legato playing. Each instrument chapter contains specific recommendations concerning tonguing syllables and their application.

The placement of the tongue stroke in the mouth has a great impact on the speed, clarity, and strength of the articulation. Consult Chapters 6 through 10 for information on the placement of the tongue during articulation. When one syllable ("tah" or "dooh," for instance) is repeated throughout a rhythmic pattern, the player is said to be "single tonguing."

Some brass teachers consider the end of the note, or release, to be part of articulation. The authors do not consider release to be part of articulation. However, the way a brass player ends notes, or releases them, is very important. Different styles of music demand different types of releases. To generalize, unless the music calls for a specific style of ending to the note, the brass player should simply stop blowing air to release a note. The tongue should not be used to create the end of a note.

Multiple Tonguing

Multiple tonguing is used when a rhythmic pattern is too fast to use the same repeated syllable. The brass player then alternates between two syllables in either a duple or a triple pattern. For example, if the rhythmic pattern is grouped in twos, fours, eights, and so on, the brass player would employ double tonguing. If the rhythms are grouped in threes, sixes, nines, and so on, the player would use triple tonguing.

Double tonguing is the alternation of two tongue syllables, such as "tah-kah." If the rhythmic pattern extends beyond two notes, the player repeats these two tongue strokes throughout the pattern ("tah-kah, tah-kah," and so on).

Triple tonguing is a group of three syllables in which one of the syllables is repeated: "tah-tah-kah." When the rhythms persist for more than three tones, the player repeats the pattern ("tah-tah-kah, tah-tah-kah," and so on). Brass players group these three syllables differently; refer to the instrument chapters for specific groupings for each instrument. As with single tonguing, the vowel sounds ("ah," "ooh," "ee") in multiple tonguing change across the range of the instrument. Advanced brass players often substitute other consonants for "t" and "k" to soften the tongue stroke. For example, the syllables "da-ga" can substitute for "tah-kah" and create a gentler tongue stroke.

Faster tonguing usually requires a faster airstream in order to produce clear and even tongue strokes.

Refer to exercises 40D, 46D, 48B, 49C, 49D, 50C, 51C, 53D for practice using double tonguing and exercises 38D, 50D, 51B, 52C, and 53C for practice using triple tonguing. More specific information on multiple tonguing is included in the instrument-specific chapters.

Common Tonguing Problems

Problems of tonguing are more similar for all the brasses than those of embouchure. The following problems occur frequently and have similar solutions on all brass instruments:

1. Too much tension in the tongue. Perhaps the most common and damaging tonguing problem, this produces a slow tongue and often an attack that is too harsh. The student should be encouraged to relax the tongue, practice slow tonguing exercises, and use less of the tongue (only the tip), in an up-and-down motion.

2. Tonguing between the teeth. This is usually incorrect, but is sometimes suggested for specific situations. This problem can usually be diagnosed by observing an accompanying jaw movement and a problem of note accuracy. The student must relearn the tongue stroke using only the tip of the tongue in an up-and-down rather than in-and-out motion.

3. Jaw movement with tongue stroke. This problem causes the same inaccuracies as does the preceding problem, but has a different source: the player is opening and closing the jaw on each tongue stroke in a chewing fashion. The player can solve this problem by firming the corners of the mouth and holding the jaw down and flat.

4. Uneven-sounding syllables during multiple tonguing. This is a very common problem, especially for those players learning multiple tonguing. Usually the "k" syllable is not as strong as the other syllable being used. The player should practice rhythms using only the weaker syllable and project a faster airstream during multiple tonguing.

Lip Slurs

Lip slurs are used when a brass player must slur between two pitches within the harmonic series that have the same fingering or are in the same position. To produce a smooth slur, the player should consider the following:

1. Changing vowel sounds during the slur aids the smoothness of the slur. Often a brass player uses an "oh" syllable for the lower note of the slur and an "ee" syllable for the upper note. This change of syllable affects the speed of the airstream and helps the lips produce the upper pitch.

2. The lip buzz must make a continuous glissando between the two pitches.

3. The air column must either remain steady or increase in velocity. Unfortunately, just the opposite is natural during a lip slur. Slowing down the airstream will either cause the higher pitch not to be produced at all or cause a break of sound between the two pitches.

4. The lip muscles must tense for an ascending lip slur and relax for a descending lip slur. The change in tension should be controlled by the corners of the mouth.

Lip slurs are a basic technique on brass instruments and should be practiced daily. Refer to exercises 7A through D, 22D, 23D, 29D, 39B, 40A, 41D, 47D, and 53A for practice of lip slurs. Chapters 6 through 10 contain further information regarding production of lip slurs on the individual brasses.

Selected Bibliography

Farkas, Philip. *The Art of Brass Playing*, Rochester, NY: Wind Music, Inc., 1962.

Kleinhammer, Edward. *The Art of Trombone Playing*, Evanston, Ill.: Summy-Birchard, 1963.

Weast, Robert. *Brass Performance*, New York: McGinnis & Marx, 1961.

5

Brass Instrument Equipment

Parts of the Brass Instruments

Each instrument of the brass family has numerous parts that the student should recognize. The chapters on the individual instruments contain labeled pictures of the instruments, but the importance of some parts is outlined here.

The leadpipe of a brass instrument is the initial piece of tubing in which the mouthpiece is inserted. The interior shape and length of this leadpipe greatly affect the sound of the instrument.

The tuning slide of a brass instrument is most often the first slide off the leadpipe. It is used for macrotuning of the instrument. Each of the valves has a movable slide as well. These slides are used for microtuning and, in the case of the trumpet, euphonium, and some tubas, are moved while playing the instrument. Lengthening any of these slides lowers the pitch of the instrument.

The valves, when depressed, allow the air column to flow through the accompanying valve slides. This causes the basic sound of the instrument and its harmonic series to be lowered in pitch.

Both the bore (the interior) and the bell of each type of instrument are available in various sizes. Chapters 6 through 10 suggest instrument sizes appropriate for various situations.

Water keys are available—in fact, standard—on most instruments. When they are opened, condensation that collects on the bore of the instrument is released. The player must be careful to maintain the cork and spring of the water key in order to provide an adequate seal when the key is closed.

Mouthpieces

Mouthpieces for brass instruments are available in literally thousands of models. The five principal mouthpiece parts that affect the sound are the following (see Figure 5–1):

Figure 5–1   Mouthpiece Nomenclature

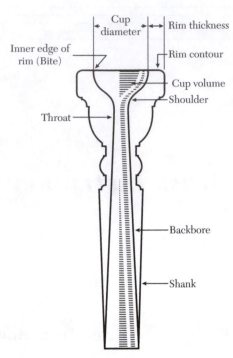

(Illustration courtesy of Yamaha Corporation of America)

1. *The rim.* Rims are available in wide, narrow, flat, and rounded shapes and in combinations of these shapes. The wider rims provide embouchure comfort but lack flexibility. Narrow rims offer good flexibility but demand embouchure strength. Rounded rims enhance the smoothness of slurs, and flatter rims provide for crisper articulations.
2. *The cup.* Depth is the most important aspect of the cup. A medium-sized cup is best. The shallower the cup, the better the upper range, but tone quality is negatively affected. Deep cups require strong embouchures but enhance the brass tone quality.
3. *The bore or throat.* These terms refer to the hole in the bottom of the cup of the mouthpiece. The smaller the bore, the more focused and small the tone quality.
4. *The backbore.* The backbore is the taper of the inside of the mouthpiece from the throat to the end of the mouthpiece. A cylindrical backbore aids in the production of the high range and produces a bright sound. A conical backbore helps the player produce a dark, full sound and loud volume.
5. *The shank.* The shank is the end of the mouthpiece that is inserted into the leadpipe. Various sizes of shanks exist for low brass instruments. The shank size must match the leadpipe size in order for the instrument to function properly. Chapters 6 through 10 each provide specific information about mouthpieces suitable for the instrument discussed. At this point, two mouthpiece brands are worthy of mention: Bach and Schilke. These two mouthpiece (and instrument) companies produce excellent mouthpieces, and over the years many other companies have used these mouthpieces as models for their own. The Bach numbering system of mouthpieces is structured so that the larger the number, the smaller the mouthpiece. The Schilke numbering system is the

opposite: the larger the number, the larger the mouthpiece. Not all the authors recommend these brands, and the reader should consult the instrument-specific chapters for further information.

Mutes

Mutes are used with brass instruments to change the timbre of the instruments and to control volume. When inserted into the brass instrument, they cause the instrument to become sharp in pitch. The player must either compensate for this or choose a "tuneable" mute that allows for compensation. The most commonly used mutes are the straight mute, the cup mute, the wah-wah mute (often referred to as the Harmon mute), and the plunger. The horn also uses a stopping mute, which is discussed in Chapter 7. Refer to Figure 5–2 for photographs of these mutes.

Miscellaneous Equipment

Each brass player should own some equipment for maintaining and cleaning the instrument. The following equipment is suggested:

1. *Valve oil.* Lightweight oil is best because it allows the valves to move quickly.
2. *Slide grease/cream.* Applied to the valve slides and tuning slides; this keeps them movable and prevents deposits from building up on the slides.
3. *Cleaning snake.* This is a flexible coil with a brush on each end used to clean the bore of the instrument.
4. *Mouthpiece brush.* This is used to clean the interior of the mouthpiece. Additional equipment is suggested in the chapters on individual instruments.

Figure 5–2   Brass Mutes

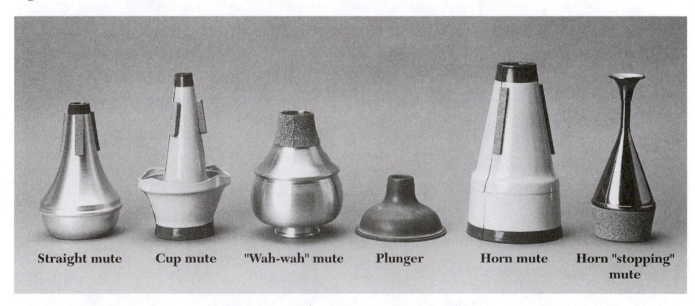

Straight mute   Cup mute   "Wah-wah" mute   Plunger   Horn mute   Horn "stopping" mute

C H A P T E R

The Trumpet

The B-flat Trumpet

The trumpet, perhaps the best-known member of the brass family, is also the highest-pitched brass instrument. The modern-day trumpet is built in a variety of keys; the most common is the B-flat trumpet. Its fundamental pitch with no valves depressed is a concert B-flat. The B-flat trumpet is a transposing instrument, sounding a major second lower than written. The parts of the B-flat trumpet are illustrated in Figure 6–1.

Figure 6–1   Parts of the Trumpet

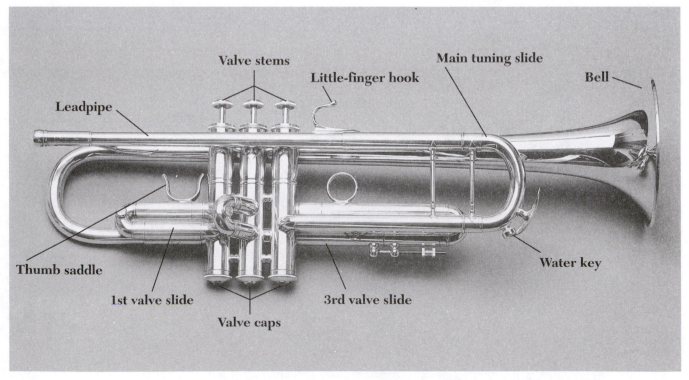

Other Instruments of the Trumpet Family

Other trumpets, pitched in various keys, have identical written ranges, and the mechanics of playing the instruments are similar. The main difference is in the size of the bore, length of the tubing, and the construction of the instrument. Figure 6–2 illustrates some instruments related to the B-flat trumpet.

Figure 6–2   Instruments of the Trumpet Family

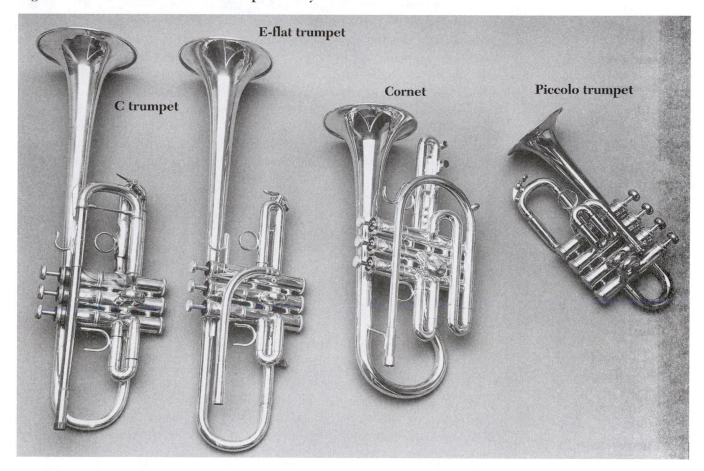

A close relative to the trumpet is the B-flat cornet. This instrument was most commonly used in American concert bands during the early decades of the twentieth century and as a beginning band instrument in the school systems. The principal difference between the cornet and the trumpet is the construction of the bore. The trumpet is primarily a cylindrical-bore instrument (the diameter of the bore remains constant until the beginning of the bell section), and the cornet has a conical bore (its bore size expands along its length). The cornet appears to be a shorter instrument because its tubing is more tightly wrapped than that of the trumpet, but it is the same length as the trumpet. In the hands of an experienced player, the cornet has a darker, more mellow tone quality than does the trumpet. For a smaller beginning student, the cornet may be easier to hold and balance than the trumpet.

The C trumpet is the trumpet of choice for most orchestral players and is also used in chamber and solo work. Smaller trumpets pitched in the keys of D, E-flat, F, G, A, and high B-flat are also used for special purposes.

Though not a true member of the trumpet family, the flügelhorn is most often used by trumpet players. Utilized primarily in jazz and commercial music, it is a conically bored, three- or four-valved instrument whose roots are in the tuba family. The flügelhorn has a much sweeter, darker sound than the trumpet or cornet.

Student Qualifications

As with any instrument, the principal qualification for playing the trumpet is a desire to be successful on it. Most persons possess the proper facial and dental characteristics to play the trumpet. However, students with facial or dental irregularities should be carefully screened. Most persons have a small overbite (that is, the top teeth protrude forward beyond the bottom teeth). Students with a large overbite or an unusual front tooth formation (especially the top teeth) should be discouraged from playing the trumpet. While it is best to avoid playing the trumpet with braces, students often have braces applied just as they begin to make progress. Many students deal with this problem by covering the braces with wax available from orthodontists. A much better solution is to use Braceguard™ or the Morgan Bumper™—devices that form a rubber guard between the lips and the braces. The important idea is to protect the lips from any damage caused by pressing them into the braces.

Another physical problem is "teardrop" lip. Some students have a small flap of flesh that hangs directly from the center of the upper lip. If large enough, this flap prevents the student from focusing air and buzzing properly. Students with these issues may be better suited for a larger-cupped brass instrument, such as trombone, euphonium, or tuba.

Proper Hand and Holding Positions

A relaxed and natural approach should be used when holding any musical instrument. In holding the trumpet, the left hand should provide the major support for the instrument. The left thumb and ring finger extend the first and third valve slides to improve intonation on certain pitches. This allows the right hand to operate the valves freely and act as a balance point. Figure 6–3 illustrates the left-hand position.

Figure 6–3
Left-hand Position

The right hand should be held so that the tips of the forefinger and the middle and ring fingers are touching the valve caps (see Figure 6–4). These fingers should be slightly curved. The right thumb should be under the leadpipe between the first and second valve casings. The little finger can be on top of the ring provided for it on the leadpipe or allowed to roam freely. Do *not* place it in the ring! This can induce tension in the hand and usually results in excessive mouthpiece pressure on the lips.

The correct sitting position for playing the trumpet is shown in Figure 6–5, and the standing position is shown in Figure 6–6.

Figure 6–4
Right-hand Position

Figure 6–5
Sitting Position

Figure 6–6
Standing Position

Embouchure Specifics

Arguably the most discussed aspect of brass playing is the embouchure. Establishing a correct embouchure during the first few lessons is critical to the success of the player. Without this foundation, which will become stronger through practice, the brass player will not be able to develop endurance, range, or flexibility. To form a correct trumpet embouchure, the student should apply the specifics listed here to the six aspects of embouchure formation listed in Chapter 3. The correct trumpet embouchure is shown in Figure 6–7.

In playing the trumpet, the oral cavity—the mouth, tongue area, glottis, and throat—must be open and relaxed. The analogies of relaxing the throat as if

Figure 6–7
Trumpet Embouchure

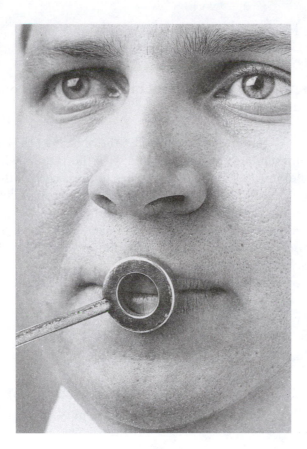

yawning or forming an "oh" syllable inside the mouth help the beginning student understand this concept. For boys, a good external check for openness in the oral cavity is the Adam's apple. If it moves up noticeably in playing, the throat is closing off the airstream.

As stated in Chapter 3, the jaw muscles should be held firm and flat. However, some jaw movement is considered essential to good tone production and flexibility on the trumpet. In general, the bottom jaw should drop when the pitch descends and close when the pitch ascends. The teeth should never close entirely or clench.

The mouthpiece and trumpet should pivot down slightly when ascending in range and pivot up when descending. This is not a technique that should be taught, but is a result of the lower jaw's smoothly adjusting to the register demands. This "pivot" will be reversed in players who have an underbite.

Unfortunately, there is no "magic" spot on the lips to place the mouthpiece. The mouthpiece should be centered over the aperture. (This can be checked by use of a mouthpiece visualizer.) For most, this is directly centered on the lips both vertically and horizontally. The mouthpiece should be placed so that an equal amount falls on both the upper and lower lips. Because no two sets of lips or teeth are alike, there are many exceptions and variations regarding mouthpiece placement. Irregular teeth, especially the top teeth, may make it uncomfortable to center the mouthpiece, or a student's natural lip buzz may be off center. The mouthpiece must not move so low on the lips that the top of the rim sits in the fleshy part of the upper lip. This inhibits the lip buzz and causes significant endurance, range, and flexibility problems.

The following exercises can be used to conceptualize the idea of controllable tension and to strengthen the embouchure muscles.

Strengthening the Embouchure Muscles: Exercises without the Mouthpiece

1. Place the thumb and forefinger on the outside of the corners of the lips. Form an embouchure. Gently push in with the fingers while using the "pulling" (smile) muscles of the embouchure to press against the fingers. Be certain to hold the chin flat and firm. This strengthens the pulling muscles.
2. Place the thumb and forefinger on the inside of the lip corners. Push the fingers outward while using the "pucker" muscles to push inward, against the fingers. Be certain that the chin remains flat. This strengthens the pucker muscles.
3. Perform both exercise 1 (for "pulling") and exercise 2 (for "pushing") in the following manner:
   a. Flex the appropriate embouchure muscles for four counts.
   b. Rest for four counts.
   c. Repeat this two-step process five times.
   d. Rest.

These exercises can be performed two or three times daily. Duration and numbers of repetitions can be increased as the muscles strengthen.

Mouthpiece Buzzing

Mouthpiece buzzing should be introduced at the first lesson. Most professional brass musicians practice regularly with the mouthpiece alone. The benefits of mouthpiece buzzing include being able to isolate tone production problems, work on ear-training, and to help focus the sound. The use of the BERP (a device used to hold the mouthpiece) is recommended. It is available for all brass instruments and is inexpensive.

Buzzing the lips alone, without the mouthpiece, is advocated by some brass teachers. This may be helpful, but is likely to be difficult and discouraging to the beginner. Lip buzzing is valuable for the advanced player who is having problems centering the tone or playing softly.

Exercises with the Mouthpiece to Strengthen the Embouchure

1. *Sirens:* Buzz the mouthpiece, making a glissando with the pitch up and down. Buzz specific intervals, ending with the octave.
2. Buzz specific scales and intervals without the siren effect. Check the pitches at a keyboard while buzzing.
3. Buzz the mouthpiece in all ranges, including the pedal range. (Pedal pitches are those pitches that exist below the written range of the instrument, below concert E in the bass clef staff.) Extend the range to pedal c.
4. Buzz the lips on exercises designed around the overtone series. See Figure 6–8 for exercises using the overtone series of the trumpet.

Figure 6–8   Lip Flexibility Exercises

Descend using all valve combinations.

Descend using all valve combinations.

Descend using all valve combinations.

Embouchure Problems

Many of the common trumpet embouchure problems and their solutions were listed in Chapter 3. Of these, the "smile" embouchure, bunched-up chin, and excessive mouthpiece pressure are the most common. One very common trumpet embouchure problem not addressed in Chapter 3 is the rolling in of the bottom lip. Both lips must roll in slightly to form a usable embouchure. However, trumpet students sometimes roll the bottom lip in too far to achieve short-term results. This will cause problems with endurance and upper-range production in the long term. The problem can easily be diagnosed by looking at the student's lower lip while playing. Have the student play an ascending chromatic scale. If all of the fleshy part of the lower lip rolls in and disappears, the student should be encouraged to "grip" the rim of the mouthpiece with the pucker muscles and firm the corner muscles. This will cause the lower lip to remain firm and not roll in.

Moderate mouthpiece pressure is required to seal the lips against air leakage. Often students apply too much pressure, particularly on the upper lip. Excessive redness, circular indentations (from the mouthpiece), or small abrasions inside the lip are all telltale signs of this problem. Proper development of the embouchure muscles and adequate breath support will help fix this problem.

Articulation

Tonguing

The basic function of the tongue in brass playing is to begin the pitch with a particular style of attack. The tongue acts as a valve to release the air and, along with the airstream, controls the length and strength of the notes.

The placement of the tongue stroke on trumpet is generally behind the upper teeth, at the top of the teeth, and near the gum line. To find this spot, the student should say the word "tip" or the syllable "tah" and notice the placement of the tip of the tongue in the mouth and the tongue's action. The tongue should pull downward when the air is released.

The tongue should be relaxed. Excess tension creates a thick, slow, unmanageable articulation. The student should use only the front part of the tongue when articulating. To relax the tongue, ask the student to produce a rolled *r* sound while articulating. This can be performed only with a relaxed tongue. Practicing with the mouthpiece alone can also help this problem.

By changing the speed and the shape of the tongue and by using different syllables, it is possible to articulate in staccato, legato, portato, or accented styles. For most trumpet articulations, the syllable "too" is recommended for use in the lower register, "tah" in the middle register, and "tee" in the upper register. Changing the syllable also raises and lowers the back of the tongue, which facilitates the change of register.

For legato articulation, the same method of tonguing should be used with a *d* sound. Use of "doo," "dah," and "dee," respectively, for the lower, middle, and upper registers moves the tongue farther back on the hard palate and produces a softer articulation.

Staccato tonguing is performed with a "dah" or "tah" articulation, depending on the desired sharpness of the attack. The difference between staccato and normal tonguing is the length of the notes, not the attack. Students should not stop the notes with the tongue.

Portato articulation is literally half staccato and half legato. Use of the "dah" syllable works well for this articulation.

Accents are played with a sharper, firmer tongue stroke and stronger air column. Marcato accents are firmer still.

Multiple Tonguing

Both double and triple tonguing should be introduced to players by the time they reach high school age.

The most commonly used pair of syllables for double tonguing on trumpet is "tah-kah." If a less aggressive, legato style is desired, the student should use "dah-gah." The "tah" and "dah" syllables are produced at the same point in the mouth as when single-tonguing. The "kah" and "gah" syllables are produced in the back of the mouth. The back of the tongue is raised against the teeth and/or the roof of the mouth and is immediately relaxed. Refer to exercises 40D, 46D, 48B, 49C, 49D, 50C, 51C, 53D for practice using double tonguing.

The same syllables are used when triple tonguing on the trumpet. The order of the syllables should be "tah-tah-kah, tah-tah-kah," and so forth. Some brass players reverse the syllables and use the sequence "tah-kah-tah" when triple tonguing. The authors do not recommend this sequence except in specific musical circumstances where the triple tongue is not intended to create a triplet feel or where there is only one triplet figure followed by a longer note. Refer to exercises 38D, 50D, 51B, 52C, and 53C for practice using triple tonguing.

The most difficult aspect of multiple tonguing on the trumpet is the production of the "kah" or "gah" syllable. As was pointed out in Chapter 4, these syllables are often softer and stuffy sounding compared with the "tah" and "dah" syllables. The student should practice tonguing passages only with the "kah" or "gah" syllable to strengthen these articulations.

Flutter tonguing is occasionally called for in advanced trumpet literature and is common in jazz. It is performed by placing the tip of the tongue on the roof of the mouth in a tonguing position. Keep the back of the tongue up and exhale while performing a rolling of the *r* sound. The tip of the tongue should remain relaxed.

Slurring

As was pointed out in Chapter 4, some types of slurs on brass instruments, called "lip slurs," require special techniques in order to perform them smoothly.

Lip slurs are best learned initially on the mouthpiece. The use of different syllables is helpful in learning to produce these types of slurs. Producing the syllables "dah-ee" when ascending and "dee-ah" when descending aids in production of the slur. In effect, this raises the back of the tongue for the upper note while lowering it for the lower pitch. The embouchure muscles must tense for the upper pitch and relax for the lower note. Refer to exercises 7A, 7B, 7C, 7D, 22D, 27A, 27B, 29A, 29D, 38A, 39A, 40A, 47D, and 53A for lip slur studies. See Figure 6–8 for basic lip slur exercises on the trumpet.

Breath Control

Breath control on the trumpet should be developed in a relaxed fashion. Other than at the embouchure, no points of resistance should be encountered by the air column. The throat, tongue, and abdominal muscles should all be relaxed during exhalation, allowing the diaphragm to fully relax.

A "breathing tube" can be used to teach relaxed inhalation. Simply a short piece of 3/4-inch PVC (polyvinyl chloride) pipe, it can be found at any hardware store. Putting one end between the teeth and breathing deeply drops the Adam's apple and opens the throat.

Beginning the First Tone

After the student has been instructed in the fundamental aspects of breathing and embouchure formation, it is time to produce the first tone. Ask the student to put the lips together as if saying the syllable "mm" or "emm," take a large breath, and blow air through the lips. Have the student do this several times so that you can check the student's breathing. This process should then be repeated with the mouthpiece alone. While exhaling a steady air column, most students produce a buzz through the mouthpiece. Those who do not should pronounce "pooh" while holding the lips in the "mm" position. The explosion of the air created by the "pooh" syllable should start the buzz. The student should inhale through the corners of the mouth with the mouthpiece already in place on the lips. The air should never be held in the body.

Once a buzz is produced, the student should manipulate the pitch up and down using the embouchure and eventually center on a pitch, possibly the second-line G in the treble clef. Using the trumpet itself at the first lesson is not recommended; students have enough new ideas to concentrate on without worrying about holding the trumpet and adding the trumpet's resistance to the creation of the buzz.

Intonation Tendencies

All brass instruments have similar intonation tendencies, but methods of compensating differ. All student trumpets will have an adjustable third valve slide. Try to encourage your students to use trumpets with an adjustable first valve slide as well. Many intonation tendencies can be corrected by extending these slides. For example, any note played with the first and third valves in combination is naturally sharp on the trumpet. To play such a pitch in tune, the student should extend either the first or the third valve slide. The following tendencies of valve combinations can be corrected by moving these slides

1	slightly sharp
1, 2	moderately sharp
1, 3	very sharp
1, 2, 3	very sharp
2, 3	slightly flat (this tendency cannot be corrected by moving slides)
3	moderately flat

The use of alternative fingerings is another method of adjusting intonation tendencies. Many pitches can be played with a variety of fingerings. By using the tendencies of the valve combinations, the trumpet player can find an alternative fingering that adjusts the pitch either up or down. Refer to the harmonic series at the end of this chapter to see alternative fingering possibilities. When studying this chart, remember that any pitch that can be played with the 1–2 valve combination can also be played with the third valve alone.

On higher-keyed trumpets, pitch problems are exaggerated. Smaller mouthpieces also tend to exaggerate intonation tendencies.

Ranges

Development of a good lower and a good upper register is the result of years of practice. It is important not to push the trumpet student into the upper reg-

Figure 6–9   The Overtone Series of the Trumpet

Figure 6–10   Suggested Register Guidelines for the Trumpet

Beginning   Intermediate   Advanced

ister too quickly. This can lead to bad habits, including excessive mouthpiece pressure and mouthpiece shifting. Because facial configurations and muscle control vary greatly, registers that come naturally to one trumpet student may take longer to develop in another. As the trumpeter ascends into the upper register he or she should focus a faster, more intense airstream, pucker the lips toward the center, keep the corners firm, and avoid excess mouthpiece pressure. As the player descends to the lower register, he or she should slow the airstream, drop the jaw, and avoid overrelaxing the embouchure. Figure 6–10 lists suggestions of registers—expectations at various experience levels on the trumpet.

Warm-up and Practice Techniques

Daily practice should be divided into two or three sessions. Dividing practice into sessions helps avoid fatigue and allows the muscles to recuperate, which is especially important for younger students whose muscles are developing. The two- to- three sessions should consist of warm-ups and technical routines, étude and solo work, and review and embouchure-building material.

The actual warming up of the lips should not take more than 10 minutes. During this time, extremes in register should be avoided. Practice should start in the middle register and gradually expand, with frequent rests.

The warm-up and technical routine should cover all aspects of trumpet playing. Warm-ups should be very structured for inexperienced players; less so for advanced players. This session can be as short as 15 minutes for the beginner or as long as 2 hours for the professional. Refer to Figure 6–11 for suggested warm-up exercises.

What is studied in the second session—étude and solo work—is self-evident. A variety of étude material stressing both technical and lyrical playing is important. Solo material should be chosen according to the ability of the student, with emphasis on musicianship. Refer to the literature lists at the end of this chapter for suggested material.

The third session, review and embouchure building, is an aspect of practice frequently overlooked. This time should be used to review materials covered during the day and to work on endurance- and range-building exercises. The student should practice until the muscles are very fatigued and then stop. This final session is important in building range and endurance.

Figure 6–11   Warm-up Exercises for the Trumpet

Sirens—play on the mouthpiece.

Repeat on all valve combinations.

Repeat on all valve combinations.

Repeat on all keys.

Repeat on all valve combinations.

Repeat on all valve combinations.

Repeat on all valve combinations.

Repeat on all valve combinations.

Figure 6–11   Continued
Extend register up and down on pattern.

A brief warm-down may be needed at the end of a particularly strenuous day. Light buzzing of the mouthpiece in and below the staff helps to gradually relax the muscles.

Specific Techniques for the Trumpet

Vibrato

The use of vibrato on the trumpet is very common. However, it is an advanced technique that should be introduced after the student can play consistently in all registers with ease. Vibrato should be used with care, as a way to enhance a melodic line.

Trumpet players use three types of vibrato. The first, "hand vibrato," is the easiest to teach. With some practice this vibrato is easily controlled. It is created by a slight movement of the right hand against the valves or valve casing, usually in a slow, rhythmic motion. Hand vibrato is especially well suited for jazz and commercial music when a wide vibrato is often desired.

"Jaw vibrato" is, perhaps, the most useful type of vibrato. Often referred to as "lip vibrato," it is actually produced by a combined movement of the lip and jaw. Moving the jaw as if saying "yah-yah" while keeping the throat and tongue relaxed produces the proper sound. Too much movement of the jaw makes the vibrato too wide and affects accuracy and intonation.

"Diaphragm vibrato" is produced by pulsating the air column and is the least used of all types of vibrato. The most difficult to teach of the three, it is not recommended for trumpet.

Lip Trills

The lip trill is a rapid change from one note to another using only the lips to change the notes. This technique is an extension of the lip slur and should not be expected of beginners. The jaw moves in a motion similar to that used in jaw vibrato. Lip trills are used only in the upper register, where the overtone partials are close together. See Chapter 7, on the horn, for further information on the production of lip trills.

The shake is a variation of the lip trill. The right hand rocks rapidly back and forth to widen the lip trill. It is used almost exclusively in jazz and commercial music.

Glissando

The glissando, drop (quick descending glissando), and doit (a short ascending glissando) are all performed with the valves partially depressed.

Transposition

All serious trumpet players will need to know how to transpose at sight in several keys and directions. The most common method of transposing for trumpet players is "note by note." In this method the player reads the written pitch up or down in the appropriate direction and interval to produce the sounding pitch. For example, a player using a B-flat trumpet but reading a C trumpet part must read all pitches up a major second. The most common transpositions stem from use of the C trumpet and include up a perfect fourth, down a minor third, and down a major second. See Chapter 7, for a list of common terms used to indicate transpositions.

Choosing a Trumpet and Trumpet Equipment

There are many brands and models of trumpets and cornets from which to choose in a variety of price ranges. The B-flat trumpet is the only instrument needed through high school. Unfortunately, not all trumpets are created equal.

Characteristics to look for in a quality beginner trumpet and accessories include the following:

1. An adjustable and offset third valve slide ring.
2. A thumb ring on the first valve slide.
3. Valves made of monel metal (more durable), rather than plated metal.
4. A trumpet case that holds the trumpet securely and has a separate compartment for mutes, oil, music, and other objects.

Recommended Trumpets

Instruments that meet these criteria (except where noted) include the following:

Recommended Beginning Trumpets

> Holton T 602 (no thumb ring)
> Yamaha YTR 2335
> Getzen 390 (no thumb ring)
> Bach 300 series

Recommended Beginning Cornets

> Yamaha YCR 2310, 2330
> Getzen 300 series, models 380 and 381

When the serious student reaches high school, he or she might consider purchasing a better trumpet. Recommended instruments for high school, collegiate, and professional players include the following:

Recommended Advanced Trumpets

> Bach, Stradivarius 180 series
> Schilke B1 through B7 series, S-22, S-32
> Yamaha 6000 and 8000 series

All of these instruments are available in a variety of bore sizes and come with a choice of different bells and leadpipes.

Trumpets built in other keys are suggested for the advanced player only. The following instruments are recommended as excellent models:

C Trumpets

> Bach, Stradivarius C180
> Yamaha YTR-8445

D/E-flat Trumpets

> Schilke E 3L
> Yamaha YTR-6610, 9620

Piccolo Trumpets

> Yamaha YTR-9810, A/B-flat trumpet
> Schilke P54, A/B-flat trumpet
> Yamaha YTR-9710, F/G trumpet
> Schilke G1L, F/G trumpet

Mouthpieces

Many trumpet manufacturers also make mouthpieces; some companies specialize only in mouthpieces. There are thousands of mouthpiece choices, but most standard mouthpieces suffice for both beginners and high school students. Larger mouthpieces generally have a more pleasing sound. The cup should be fairly deep with a slightly rounded rim. As the student progresses, wider and deeper mouthpieces can be used to help increase volume and control, as well as improve tone quality.

Standard mouthpieces that work well with beginning through high school students include the following:

Recommended Mouthpieces

> Bach 3C, 5C, 7C
> Schilke 11, 12, 14A4
> Yamaha 11C4, 15, 16C4

Mutes

The trumpet utilizes more types of mutes than any other brass instrument. Mutes are called for in virtually every style of music and are available in several price ranges. By the time they reach high school, all students should own several mutes, including a straight mute, a cup mute, and a wah-wah mute. The following manufacturers produce excellent mutes for trumpet:

Recommended Mutes for Trumpet

> Tom Crown (straight mute)
> Vincent Bach (straight mute)
> Denis Wick (straight mute)
> Humes and Berg (cup mute)
> Harmon (wah-wah mute)
> Jo-Ral (wah-wah mute)

Cleaning and Maintaining the Trumpet

A trumpet player should clean the instrument at least four times per year. It should be cleaned in a large sink or tub that is big enough to fully immerse the body of the trumpet. The following cleaning supplies are needed:

> Mouthpiece brush
> Valve brush
> Flexible snake brush
> Cleaning rod and cheesecloth
> Slide grease
> Valve oil
> Mild dishwashing detergent
> Warm water

To disassemble the trumpet for cleaning, remove the tuning slide, valve slides, and bottom valve caps and soak them in warm water. Remove the three valves and set them aside on a soft towel. Place the body of the trumpet into the warm water and let it soak.

Never put the entire valve assembly under water when cleaning. Dip the valves in the water far enough to cover the valve itself, making sure that the pads or felts are kept dry. Rinse with clean water and carefully dry with a soft cloth. Put the valves aside while cleaning the rest of the trumpet.

Use the flexible snake to clean each valve slide and the main tuning slide. Take care not to force the snake around the tight bend in each of the valve slides or it may become stuck. Flush the slides with clean water and then dry them.

Carefully run the flexible snake brush down each of the tubes of the bell of the trumpet, taking care not to scratch the inner wall of the valve casings. The leadpipe naturally collects the most debris, and extra time should be taken in cleaning it.

Wrap a piece of cheesecloth around the cleaning rod and carefully swab out each of the valve casings. Remember that the slightest dent or scratch can cause a valve to stick.

Reassemble the trumpet, starting with the valves. Be careful not to touch the valve itself; handle it by the valve stem or cap. Coat each valve with a liberal amount of valve oil and place it back in the proper valve casing, taking care to align the valve guide with the corresponding groove in the valve casing.

Grease and reassemble the slides. To do this, place a small amount of slide grease on the slide and spread it on the slide with the fingers. Depress the appropriate valve so as not to build up any undue pressure, and put the slide into the trumpet. Wipe off any excess grease.

The mouthpiece should be cleaned regularly with a mouthpiece brush. Some manufacturers offer leadpipe swabs. Consisting of a small chamois or cloth attached to a weighted string, they are to be pulled through the leadpipe and tuning slide after each use.

The exterior of a lacquer-finished trumpet needs little maintenance. Wipe off gently with soap and warm (NOT HOT) water. For silver or nickel-plated instruments, use a nonabrasive polish to shine the finish.

History of the Trumpet

The modern trumpet has been in existence since approximately 1860. Prior to 1860, the trumpet underwent significant changes to reach its present form.

The trumpet's early history can be traced to signaling devices such as the conch shell, animal horn, and shofar. As the science of metallurgy progressed, these signaling devices were made of metal and lengthened in order to play more pitches. One of the earliest examples of the natural trumpet is a set found in the tomb of King Tutankhamen. These early trumpets were limited to playing only the notes of the overtone series. If the fundamental pitch of a trumpet was a D, as was common in the Baroque period, that trumpet could play only those pitches in the D overtone series. Consequently, trumpets were built in different keys, or extra coiled tubing called "crooks" were added to lengthen the trumpet and change its overtone series.

The late-Baroque period represents the high point of the natural trumpet. The instrument was recognized as a virtuoso solo instrument. Because of the high register commonly used, much of the repertory from this period is demanding to perform, even on modern instruments.

Development of the trumpet centered on attempts to chromaticize the instruments. One instrument related to the trumpet is the cornetto. This instrument represented a cross between a brass instrument and a recorder. Usually constructed of wood and leather, the cornetto combined the fingering system of the recorder with the cup-shaped mouthpiece of the trumpet. It was used extensively from the Renaissance through the early Baroque period.

As composers began to experiment with chromaticism, the natural trumpet fell into disuse. In the late eighteenth century, an attempt at adding chromatics to the trumpet created the keyed trumpet and later, the keyed bugle. Utilizing four to twelve clarinetlike keys, these keyed instruments could perform more chromatic music. Two standard concerti were written for the keyed trumpet: the Concerto in E-flat by Haydn and the Concerto in E by Hummel. The most significant change to the trumpet came with the invention of the valve, circa 1815. Many different valve systems have been tried, but the modern trumpet generally uses piston valves. The acceptance of valved brasses in orchestras took decades, but bands quickly took advantage of the new instrument.

Graded Literature Lists

Method Books, Beginning

Edwards/Hovey	Method for Cornet or Trumpet
Feldstein	Yamaha Band Student
Getchell	First Book of Practical Studies
Hering	The Beginning Trumpeter
Kinyon	Breeze-Easy Method
Wallace	First Book of Trumpet Solos

Method Books, Intermediate

Arban	Complete Conservatory Method
Clarke	Setting Up Drills
Concone (Sawyer)	Lyrical Studies
Gower	Rubank Advanced Method
Hering	40 Progressive Studies
Hering	32 Études
Hickman	Trumpet Lessons
Irons	27 Groups of Exercises
Vandercook	Études
Voxman	Selected Studies

Method Books, Advanced

Bai Lin	Lip Flexibilities
Bitsch	20 Études
Brandt	34 Studies
Charlier	36 Études Transcendante
Clarke	Technical Studies
Gekker	Articulation Studies
Gates	Odd Meter Études
Goldman	Practical Studies
Nagel	Speed Studies
Schlossberg	Daily Drills and Technical Studies
Vizzutti	Trumpet Method, Vol. 1–3

Grade 1 Solo Literature

Barnes	Clifford Barnes Trumpet Album
Franck	Panis Angelicus
Froseth	The Individualized Instructor: Solos
Hartzell	A Trumpeter's Prayer
Hering	Classic Pieces for the Advancing Trumpeter
Isacoff	Skill Builders for Trumpet
Smith	Firefly
Smith	Picnic Time
Vandercook	Lyra
Vincent	Air for Cornet

Grade 2 Solo Literature

Bach	Aria, Bist du bei mir
Bartok	Evening in the Country
Fitzgerald	English Suite
Laburda	Peter with Trumpet
Maltby	Ceremonial March
Naulais	Promenade Lyonnaise
Poot	Humoresque
Telemann	Suite No. 1
Vandercook	Trumpet Stars, vol. 1 and 2
Voxman	Concert and Contest Collection
Williams	Little Classics

Grade 3 Solo Literature

Anderson	Trumpeter's Lullaby
Bernstein	Rondo for Lifey
Burke	Magic Trumpet
Clarke, H.	Ten Solos for Cornet
Clarke, J.	Trumpet Voluntary
Hovhaness	Prayer for St. Gregory
Nelhybel	Suite for Trumpet and Piano
Scarlatti/Fitzgerald	Scarlatti Suite
Wastall	Baroque Music for Trumpet
Young	Contempora Suite

Grade 4 Solo Literature

Balay	Petite Pièce Concertante
Balay	Andante and Allegretto
Bovinette (ed.)	Arban's The Art of Phrasing
Bozza	Badinage
Clarke, H.	Stars in a Velvety Sky
Corelli	Sonata opus 5, no.8
Fitzgerald	Gaelic Suite
Handel	Aria con Variazioni
Mager (ed.)	Nine Grand Solos
Nagel	Baroque Music for Trumpet
Purcell	Sonata
Ropartz	Andante and Allegro
Shostakovich	Polka, from "The Age of Gold"

Grade 5 Solo Literature

Barat	*Andante and Scherzo*
Buesser	*Variations in D-flat*
Clarke	*The Debutante*
Fiocco	*Allegro*
Goedicke	*Concert Étude*
Howarth	*The Amazing Mr. Arban*
Kaminski	*Concertino for Trumpet and Strings*
Jolivet	*Air de Bravoure*
Shakhov	*Scherzo*
Staigers	*Carnival of Venice*
Starer, R.	*Invocation*
Thomé, F.	*Fantasie*
Turrin	*Caprice*
Viviani	*Two Sonatas*

Grade 6 Solo Literature

Arnold	*Fantasy*
Arutunian	*Concerto*
Bozza	*Caprice*
Enesco	*Légende*
Gallagher	*Sonata*
Goldman	*Scherzo*
Haydn	*Concerto in E-flat*
Hindemith	*Sonate*
Honegger	*Intrada*
Hummel	*Concerto in E-flat*
Kennan	*Sonata*
Riisager	*Concertino*
Stevens	*Sonata*
Tomasi	*Concerto*

Selected Discography

André, Maurice
> *Ultimate Trumpet Collection*, Erato 92861

Dokshitser, Timofei
> *Poème*, Marcophon 916

Eklund, Niklas
> *Art of the Baroque Trumpet, vol. 3*, Naxos 553735

Hardenberger, Hakan
> *Virtuoso Trumpet*, Bis 287

Hickman, David
> *David Hickman, Trumpet*, Crystal CD 668

Marsalis, Wynton
> *Carnaval*, Sony 42137

Mase, Raymond
> *Trumpet Vocalise*, Summit 210

Nakariakov, Sergei
> *Concertos for Trumpet*, Teldec 94554

Schwarz, Gerard
> *Cornet Favorites and Hits*, Nonesuch 79157

Smith, Philip
> *Contest Solos for Young Trumpeters*, ITG CD 111

Smithers, Donald
> *Trumpet Concertos*, Philips 9500-109

Stevens, Thomas
> *Thomas Stevens, Trumpet*, Crystal CD 761

Selected Bibliography

Altenburg, J. E. *Trumpet and Kettledrummers' Art*, Nashville, TN: The Brass Press, 1974.

Baines, Anthony. *Brass Instruments: Their History and Development*, Mineola, NY: Dover Publications, 1993.

Farkas, Philip. *The Art of Brass Playing*, Rochester, NY: Wind Music, 1989.

Frederiksen, Brian. *Arnold Jacobs: Song and Wind*, Gurnee, IL: Windsong Press, 1996.

Johnson, Keith. *Brass Performance and Pedagogy*, Upper Saddle River, NJ: Prentice-Hall, 2002.

Sherman, Roger. *Trumpeter's Handbook*, North Greece, NY: Accura Music, 1979.

Smithers, Donald. *The Music and History of the Baroque Trumpet before 1721*, Nashville, TN: The Brass Press, 1988.

Tarr, Edward. *The Trumpet*, Portland, OR: Amadeus Press, 1988.

Harmonic Series, Trumpet (2nd partials)

Fingering Chart, Trumpet

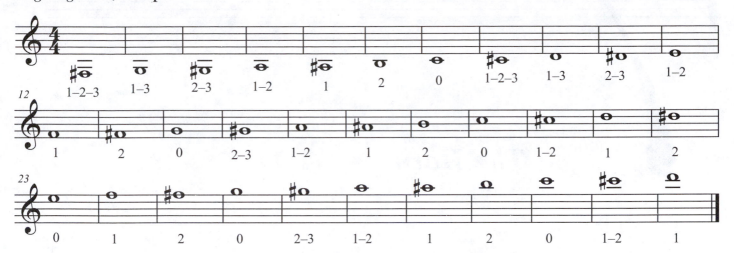

7

The Horn

The horn is the most versatile member of the brass family. It is equally at home in an orchestra, a band, and a woodwind or brass quintet. Its conical construction and conical mouthpiece give the horn a darker sound than the other brass instruments. This smoothness of timbre has endeared the horn to composers of the eighteenth, nineteenth, and twentieth centuries. The horn most used today is pitched in F, sounding a perfect fifth lower than written. The horn and its parts are illustrated in Figure 7–1.

Instruments of the Horn Family

The instruments related to the horn consist of variations of the basic instrument. The "natural" (valveless) horn has recently regained popularity. It is limited to the pitches available in its overtone series. This can be compensated for by inserting a longer or shorter slide, or crook, which will provide a different overtone series. Orchestral composers of the Romantic era, when writing four horn parts, would often pair the first and second horns in one key and the third and fourth horns in another. This system allowed for the horn section to play twice as many notes as a section of horns all using the same overtone series. In most ensemble music employing four horns, the first and third horn parts are "high" horn parts, and the second and fourth parts are "low" parts.

Two types of horns are generally in use today, although a number of varieties exist. These two instruments are the single horn pitched in F and the standard double horn pitched in F/B-flat. (shown in Figure 7–1). The single horn is lighter in weight and has fewer slides to maintain and fewer fingerings to use than the double horn (see Figure 7–1a). The double horn is used most often and has the advantage of having two overtone series available. This allows for a number of alternative fingerings (given at the end of the chapter) that can aid in solving intonation and technical problems. The double horn also

Figure 7–1   Parts of the Double Horn

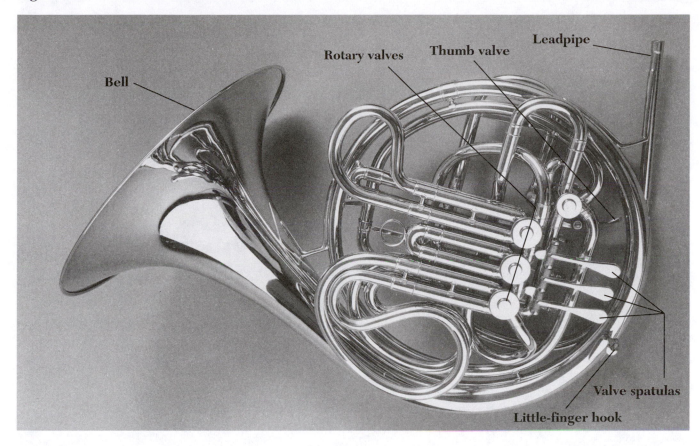

fills in the gaps that exist in the chromatic scale in the lowest register of the single horn and, of most value, makes the upper-register notes easier to play by using the B-flat side of the horn.

The B-flat side of the horn is employed on A-flat within the staff and higher. The tone quality produced by the B-flat horn below this note is less desirable than that produced on the F side. Other horns in use today include the single F horn, the single B-flat horn, the descant (B-flat and high F) horn, triple horns (F, B-flat, high F), the B-flat/high B-flat horn, and various other compensating instruments.

Student Qualifications

The nature of the horn is such that the player needs to have exceptional hearing skills. Because beginning hornists will not have the embouchure to reach most pitches without some labor, it is essential that they be able to hear the pitch to aid in playing it. As with any brass instrument, a severe over- or underbite is a hindrance in developing a good embouchure. Ideally, the teeth should be even.

Figure 7–1a   The Single F Horn

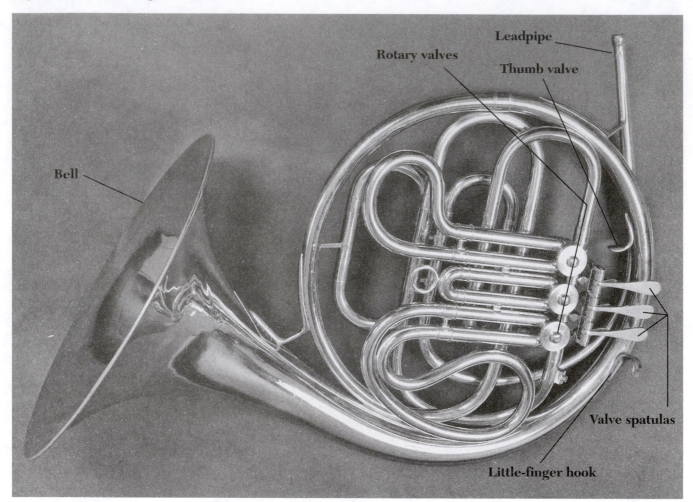

Many bands are blessed with an abundance of flutes and trumpets. Success can be attained in switching students from these instruments to horn. To play the horn, trumpet players need to modify the mouthpiece placement and the embouchure and, perhaps more important, their concept of tone. Flutists can be switched to horn with relative ease. The embouchure muscle development is similar, there is no corresponding placement problem, and the fingers of the left hand have already developed flexibility. The primary concern is to get the ex-flutist to use enough air to fill up the horn.

Proper Hand and Holding Positions

The proper position for holding and playing the horn can be divided into five steps:

1. The player should be seated. The player should sit in an erect but natural position away from the back of the chair, with both feet resting flat on the floor, the left slightly ahead of the right.

2. Bell placement depends on the size of the player. The bell should rest on the right leg, pointing slightly to the right of the body, never directly into it. If a player is uncommonly tall or short, the bell should be held off the leg.

3. The right hand goes in the bell so as to deflect the sound, not muffle it (see Figure 7–2). This is a very important but often neglected point. The right hand serves to soften the natural coarseness of the open horn, helps control intonation, and helps to support the horn while holding it. The right hand should be slightly cupped, with the fingers and thumb resting together, side by side. It should be placed in the bell on the wall away from the body at approximately "three" or "four o'clock." In playing with the bell off the leg, the hand position is the same. The weight of the horn should rest on the first knuckle of the thumb and the last joint of the index finger. This hand position will also allow the hornist to play "stopped" horn (see the explanation in the section "Specific Techniques for the Horn") by simply closing the hand.

   Manufacturers realize that the hornist will be inserting the hand in the bell, thus lowering the pitch approximately a quarter tone. To compensate for this, the horn maker builds the horn slightly sharp. Pitch can be raised or lowered by opening and closing the hand, or moving the hand in or out of the bell. The farther a player inserts the hand into the bell, the flatter the pitch becomes.

Figure 7–2
Right-hand Position

4. The fingers of the left hand rest on the valve spatulas (see Figure 7–3). The little finger should rest in the finger ring, and the ring, middle, and index fingers each should rest lightly on the valve spatulas. The fingers should be slightly curved. Contact with the spatulas should be maintained at all times, with the fingers never allowed to point up in the air. The thumb should be on the B-flat trigger if a double horn is used, or in the thumb ring if a single horn is used.

Figure 7–3   Left-hand Position

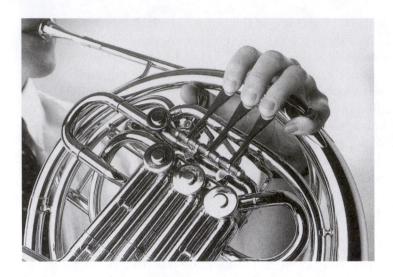

5. Bring the horn to the head, not the head to the horn. Too often the beginner sets the bell of the horn on the leg and allows it to dictate the playing position. The leadpipe should angle down slightly from the mouth. The student should sit and play in as natural a position as possible (see Figure 7–4).

Figure 7–4   Sitting Position

Embouchure Specifics

The single most important factor for the beginning hornist is the embouchure. The majority of problems encountered by young hornists, including those entering college, are due to a faulty embouchure.

Forming the Horn Embouchure

To form a horn embouchure

1. The player should place the mouthpiece in the center of the lips horizontally and with the mouthpiece two-thirds on the upper lip and one-third on the lower lip.
2. The chin should be firm and flat with the jaw slightly forward.
3. The corners of the mouth should be firm and should push toward the center of the mouthpiece.
4. The lips should be slightly pursed, or puckered.
5. The oral cavity should be open, with no resistance points to the air column.
6. The lips should be moist.
7. The lower jaw should drop noticeably as the hornist descends into the lower register.

Figure 7–5 illustrates the embouchure for the horn.

**Figure 7–5
Embouchure
of the Horn**

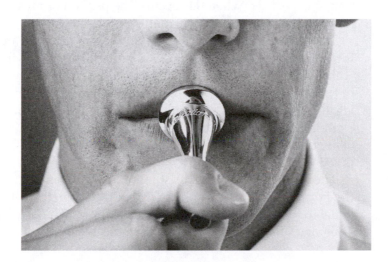

Embouchure Problems

Embouchure problems outlined in Chapter 3 are very common on horn. In addition to those listed there, you may often see a student using too much pucker in the embouchure. This results in a thick, tubby, airy sound. The student should firm the corners of the mouth to correct this problem and drop the lower jaw.

Another very common embouchure problem on horn is the use of a trumpet embouchure. This is usually caused by switching a player from trumpet to horn and often results in a poor low range and a thin, constricted tone. On the horn, the student must reposition the mouthpiece higher on the top lip and use more pucker than with a trumpet embouchure.

Articulation

Tonguing

Starting the note correctly is a technique that can and should be taught immediately. The proper syllable to use when single tonguing on the horn is "too." The tongue should touch the back of the upper teeth where they meet the gum. The tongue movement should be kept to a minimum and should be an up-and-down motion. The tongue should lightly "flick" into the air column. Never allow the student to tongue between the teeth. Many hornists use a tongue position that is too high, resulting in an attack that is harsh and, if the tongue is high enough, results in a disruption of the airstream. The hornist should use a "doo" syllable when playing a legato passage. Refer to exercises 9C, 9D, 10A, 10B, 11B, 13A, 13C, 15B, 16B, 21D, and 22C for practice using single tonguing.

Multiple Tonguing

Certain passages in music require notes to be articulated faster than single tonguing permits. When this occurs, the performer must either double or triple tongue, depending upon the grouping of the notes.

The syllables to use for double tonguing on the horn are "tuh-kuh." The performer must produce the "kuh" syllable farther back in the mouth than the "tuh." The same syllables should be used when triple tonguing on the horn, but in the following order: "tuh-kuh-tuh, tuh-kuh-tuh," and so forth. For a more legato attack, the student should change the "t" to "d" and the "k" to "g".

Refer to exercises 40D, 46D, 48B, 49C, 49D, 50C, 51C, 53D for practice using double tonguing. Refer to exercises 38D, 50D, 51B, 52C, and 53C for practice using triple tonguing.

The same problems that exist in multiple tonguing for the trumpet occur on the horn. The principal problem is that the strength of the *k* or *g* syllable is unequal to that of the *t* or *d*. Refer to Chapter 6, "The Trumpet," under "Multiple Tonguing," for exercises to strengthen this syllable.

Beginning the First Tone

To start the initial note, the student should first buzz on the mouthpiece. Stressing a relaxed embouchure and a steady airflow, the teacher should buzz and have the student imitate the pitch. This is the optimum time to emphasize playing in the center of the pitch and the correct use of the air. As soon as the student can achieve a relaxed buzz on the mouthpiece, he or she should try it on the horn, starting on a second-line G in the treble clef. The embouchure should be relaxed and supported by the airstream.

The Overtone Series of the Horn

Knowledge of the overtone series is essential for the hornist to understand the intricacies of the fingering system. The harmonic series of the horn in F is reproduced in Figure 7–6. The higher one plays in an overtone series, the closer together the partials. The upper-register pitches tend to be easier to play on the B-flat horn because the partials are farther apart.

Figure 7–6   The Overtone Series of the Horn

Intonation Tendencies

Hornists rarely use the 1–3 or 1–2–3 valve combinations because of the large number of alternative fingerings available on the double horn. In fact, only two pitches must be played with these combinations and have no other fingerings: bottom-line G natural and G-flat in the bass clef. Most intonation tendencies are compensated for by the use of alternative fingerings. The student should consult the F and B-flat horn harmonic series charts at the end of this chapter for alternative fingerings.

Tuning the horn is a much more involved process than tuning any other brass instrument. To tune the horn, play third-space C in the treble clef on the open F horn and check it with an electronic tuner. Next, play third-line B natural to check the second valve slide; then play B-flat to check the first valve slide and A for valves 1 and 2 in combination. Remember that the 1–2 combination is naturally sharp and that pulling the first or second valve slide to compensate for the A will make the B or B-flat change in pitch. It is better to adjust the pitch with the right hand or lip tension. Next, play A-flat with the 2–3 combination to check the third valve slide. Repeat this procedure on the B-flat side of the horn by starting on top-line F and descending chromatically.

Most horns have a number of tuning slides in addition to the valve slides. The first slide off the leadpipe is the combination slide and will tune the entire horn. Check which side of the double horn other slides affect by pulling them out one by one and blowing through the horn. Pull a slide completely out of the horn and play a note on the F side of the horn. If a true note sounds, the slide is a B-flat slide. If a buzz is produced, it is an F slide. Repeat this process until all the slides have been identified. Many horns have two F slides. In this case, push one all the way in and use it only as a means to empty water; tune with the other. Horns in a band should tune to a concert F instead of a concert B-flat. Tuning to concert B-flat tunes only the first valve slide.

Ranges

The development of both dependable high and low ranges is a facet of horn playing that is too often neglected. The most important idea to stress is that a hornist needs facility in all registers of the instrument.

A good high register must be developed by diligent practice. A dependable high B-flat will not "happen" until after the student has played hundreds of high Bs and Cs. There is no upper end to the range of the horn. A high register that sounds pinched or brittle, or one that is noticeably sharp, is usually the result of a smile embouchure. As the hornist ascends into the upper register, he or she should provide intense, firm air support and contract the corners of the mouth inward.

The low register of the horn often receives little attention. To practice the low register, the hornist can play easy études one octave lower than written and later move to more advanced studies. All hornists need to be able to read in bass clef. To play in the low register, the hornist must drop the lower jaw and project it slightly forward. When articulating in the low register, the player should not tongue between the teeth.

Figure 7–7 shows suggested register guidelines for the horn for players from beginning to advanced.

Figure 7–7   Suggested Register Guidelines for the Horn

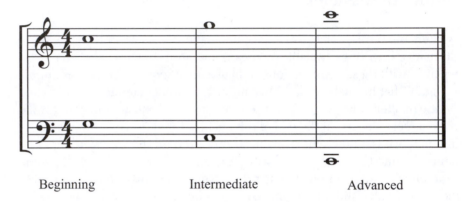

Beginning   Intermediate   Advanced

Warm-up and Practice Techniques

A good warm-up is a necessity for brass players. Usually, the beginner has only a few moments before rehearsal to prepare. To warm up, the hornist should stay in the middle register and play at a moderate dynamic level using all or selections of the warm-up exercises in Figure 7–8. It is imperative that the hornist take the mouthpiece completely away from the lips during the rests.

Figure 7–8   Warm-up Exercises for Horn

Specific Techniques for the Horn

Stopped Horn

Composers use stopped horn to produce a timbral effect. The key to playing stopped horn is in the correct positioning of the right hand. If the hand is in the right place, the hornist should need only to close the hand completely and firmly to stop the air from escaping. The fingers should be together, with the palm pressing firmly against the wall of the bell. A good stopped horn sound should "sizzle" and takes much more air than playing an open horn.

Because there is much more resistance than normal when playing stopped horn, missed notes occur more frequently. To compensate, the students must use more air and a softer tongue when articulating on stopped horn.

Playing stopped horn raises the pitch one half step, forcing the hornist to compensate by fingering all pitches one half step lower than written. Stopped horn should be played only on the F side of the horn. Stopping mutes, commonly called "brass" or "wineglass mutes," are available and greatly aid the player in dynamic control, pitch, accuracy, and evenness of timbre.

Common Terms for Muted and Stopped Horns

English	German	French	Italian
muted	gedämpft	avec sourdine	con sordino
stopped	gestopft	bouché	chiuso
	mit Dämpfer		

The symbol + over a note indicates stopped horn and o means open horn.

Lip Trills

For the hornist, when the interval to be trilled is a major second, a lip trill is in order. In producing the lip trill, the tongue aids by a fast alternation of the syllables "oh-ee-oh-ee," and so forth. This technique is an extension of the lip slur and can be practiced by using the exercises shown in Figure 7–9.

Vibrato

Whether the hornist should use vibrato is an ongoing debate. The only type of vibrato suggested for the horn player is "lip" vibrato. This is produced by a slight movement of the jaw in a "yah-yah" motion.

Figure 7–9   Lip Trill Exercises

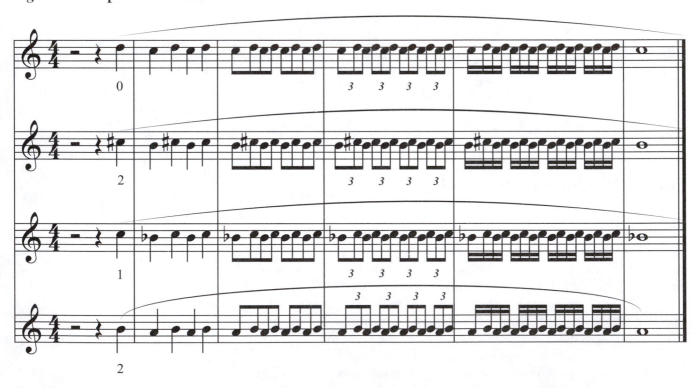

Perform the same exercises using the following pitches and fingering.

Transposition

Horn players must be able to transpose at sight in a variety of keys. The most common method of transposition on the horn is by interval and key signature adjustment. For example, to transpose to horn in E-flat (common in band march music), the player must lower all written pitches a major second. As an alternative, the player can lower all written pitches by one position on the staff and add two flats to or subtract two sharps from the key signature.

Certain transpositions, most notably B-flat, may be accompanied by the terms basso (below) or alto (above), indicating whether the notes should be raised or lowered.

Common Terms Used to Indicate Transpositions

English	German	French
F	F	fa
E	E	mi
E-flat	Es	mi-bémol
D	D	re
D-flat	Des	re-bémol
C	C	ut
B	H	si
B-flat	B	si-bémol
A	A	la
A-flat	As	la-bémol
G	G	sol
F-sharp	Fis	fa-dièse

Choosing a Horn and Horn Equipment

Choosing a horn for a school or a student can be confusing. There are many makes and models from which to choose. The three most common horns are the double horn in F/B-flat, the single F horn, and the single B-flat horn. The following horns are recommended as excellent instruments:

Recommended Horns

Yamaha

YHR 322	Single B-flat, beginner horn, extra A stop valve, .472 bore, small bell throat
YHR 314	Single F, beginner horn, .472 bore, small bell throat
YHR 567	Double horn, brass, .472 bore, medium bell throat
YHR 667	Double horn, brass, "Geyer" wrap, .472 bore, medium-large bell throat
YHR 668	Double horn, brass or silver, "Kruspe" wrap, .472 bore, medium-large bell throat

Holton

Farkas 179	Double horn, nickel silver, .468 bore, standard bell throat
Farkas 180	Double horn, brass, .468 bore, standard bell throat
Farkas 181	Same horn as 180 but with rose brass

Conn

8D	Double horn, nickel silver, .468 bore, large bell throat
8DR	Same horn as 8D but with rose brass bell, branch and lead pipe
10D	Double horn, brass, "Geyer" wrap, .468 bore, standard bell throat
10DR	Same horn as 10D but with rose brass bell, branch and lead pipe

Mouthpieces

Most standard mouthpieces will suffice for both beginners and high school students. Mouthpieces come in a variety of shapes, sizes, and rim specifications. Bigger is usually better. General characteristics to consider when choosing a mouthpiece include the following:

Rim

Wide	Increases endurance.
Narrow	Improves flexibility and range.
Round	Improves comfort.
Sharp	Increases brilliance and precision of attack.

Cup

Large	Increases volume and control.
Small	Eases fatigue.
Deep	Darkens timbre.
Shallow	Brightens sound and improves response.

Throat

Large	Increases blowing freedom, volume, and tone.
Small	Increases resistance, endurance, and brilliance.

Recommended Mouthpieces for the Horn

Holton Farkas	MDC (medium deep cup)
Holton Farkas	DC (deep cup)
Conn 5N	
Conn 5W	
Conn 7N	
Conn 7W	
Yamaha 30C4	
Yamaha 31D4	

Mutes

Many custom mutes are made, but for school use, the standard Humes and Berg Stone Lined mute is excellent. The advanced player may use mutes made by Trumcor, Lewis, and Marcus Bonna. Denis Wick, Stonelined, and Tom Crown all make a reliable model stopping mute. Plastic mutes should be avoided.

When inserting a mute into the bell, use only a slight twist to make it fit snugly. The pitch of the mute may be raised or lowered by filing or padding the corks, respectively. Attach a cord to the bottom of the mute so that it can be hung from the wrist to facilitate quick mute changes.

Cleaning and Maintaining the Horn

The best care of any instrument is preventive maintenance. From the beginning, the importance of proper care for a horn must be stressed. The student should be familiar with the correct method of emptying slides, greasing slides, oiling the valves, and restringing a valve.

Twice per year the horn should be cleaned thoroughly, and the leadpipe should be swabbed at least twice per month. To clean the horn, soak it in a tub of **lukewarm** water with a mild detergent. Remove all the slides and wipe off the excess grease. Let the horn soak for 10 minutes and then rotate it so that the water moves entirely through the horn. Remove, rinse, and dry immediately. Regrease the slides and oil the valves.

To empty water from the valve slides, hold the horn firmly, depress the valves, and gently pull out the necessary slides. Tilt the slides so that the water pours out the end of the sleeve. Most of the water accumulates in the main slide, but water often collects in the valve slides, especially in the third valve slide.

Oiling the Rotary Valves

A rotary valve should be oiled in two places: on the top and at the bottom of the valve. To oil the top, unscrew the valve cap and place a few drops of oil on the shaft of the valve. To oil the bottom of the valve, place a few drops of the oil in the crack of the spindle bearing shaft. See Figure 7–10.

Figure 7–10
Rotary Valve

Restringing the Horn Rotary Valve

The valve strings on a horn should be periodically replaced. To do so, loosen small screws C and E (see Figure 7–11). Cut approximately 8 inches of valve string, or fishing line that does not stretch, and tie a knot in one end large enough so that it will not pass through the hole in the rod (A). Starting on the outside of the valve, thread the string toward the valve. With the rotor stem to the left of the rod, wind the string around small screw C in a clockwise direction. Continue around the rotor stem (B) to the hole near the end of the rod (D). Thread the string through this hole and loop it under the head of the small screw on rod (E) in a clockwise direction. Next, pull the string taut and tighten screw E enough to hold the lever in place. Position the lever so that the string rod is parallel to the rotor casing top. Tighten screw C. When the rotor stem is to the right of the rod, the stringing steps should be reversed.

Figure 7–11   Restringing the Valve

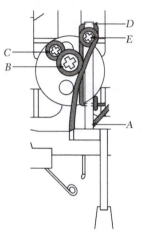

(Illustration courtesy of Yamaha Corporation of America)

A horn repair kit for the music teacher should include valve oil, slide grease, braided 30- to 50-pound test fishing line, a leadpipe cleaner, a rubber mallet, a mouthpiece puller, bumper cork or neoprene, pliers, screwdrivers, and a single-edged razor blade.

History of the Horn

The horn's early history can be traced to the primitive shofar, bucina, lituus, and others. However, the hunting horn of central Europe had a much greater impact on the development of today's horn. These early predecessors of the horn were used to conduct the hunts of the aristocracy in an orderly fashion. Different calls were used to identify the various kinds of prey and to signal the start and end of the hunt.

As was true of the trumpet of the late Renaissance, the longer horns were curved for ease of handling. This curving became central to the horn's development because the curved horn placed the bell nearer the player's hand. This allowed the hornist to bring the hand into the bell. As players inserted the hand into the bell, they found that the pitch could be altered. The Dresden hornist Hampel was instrumental in developing this concept.

The horn's progress was advanced by the invention of the valve in about 1815. With the development of the valve, the demands on the horn dramatically changed. Some composers, most notably the French, eschewed this development and continued to write for the natural horn. However, composers gradually recognized the possibilities of the valved horn. As the Romantic period progressed and composers further explored chromatic tonalities, the valved horn made irreversible gains.

The horn is often incorrectly referred to as the "French horn." During the 1500s, the British royalty imported musicians from the continent for many functions. The horn players from France apparently were referred to as "those fine French horn players." People failed to realize that the term "French" referred to the hornists' nationality, not their instruments. The United States is the only country that still refers to the horn as the French horn.

Graded Literature Lists

Method Books, Beginning

Clevenger	*The Dale Clevenger French Horn Method*
Goldstein	*A First Book of Études for Horn*
Homer	*Primary Studies for Horn*
Howe	*Method for French Horn*
Ployhar	*French Horn Study*
Pottag-Hovey	*French Horn Method*
Tuckwell	*Fifty First Exercises for Horn*

Method Books, Intermediate

Concone	*Lyrical Studies for Horn*
Endresen	*Supplementary Studies for Horn*
Getchell	*Practical Studies for Horn*
Krol	*Waldhorn Studien*
Little	*Embouchure Builder for Horn*
Maxime-Alphonse	*200 Modern Études (vols. 1 and 2)*
Schantl/Pottag	*Preparatory Melodies to Solo Work for Horn*

Method Books, Advanced

Bitsch	*12 Études*
Bozza	*18 Études en Forme d'Improvisation*
Chaynes	*15 Studies for Horn*
Gallay	*40 Preludes, op. 27*
Hackleman	*34 Characteristic Études*
Kopprasch	*60 Selected Studies*
Maxime-Alphonse	*200 Modern Horn Études (vols. 3 and 4)*
Pottag	*French Horn Passages*
Pottag/ Andraud	*Progressive and Technical Studies for French Horn*
Shoemaker	*Legato Études for Horn*

Grade 1 Solo Literature

Ameller	*Prelude*
Bray/Green	*Solos for Schools*
Hauser	*At the Fair*
Hauser	*Soldier's Song*
Hauser	*Twilight Thoughts*
Hauser	*Woodland Memories*

Jones   *First Solos for the Horn Player*
Kofron   *10 Little Compositions*
Lawton   *The Young Horn Player*
Maganini   *An Ancient Greek Melody*
Phillips   *Classical and Romantic Horn
                 Album*
Weber   *The Mighty Major*

Grade 2 Solo Literature

Ameller   *Canzone*
Ameller   *Rondo*
Bakaleinikoff   *Canzona*
Bakaleinikoff   *Cavatina*
Ballatore   *Serenata*
Benson   *Soliloquy*
Corelli, A.   *Sonata in F Major*
Maganini   *Song of the Chinese Fisherman*
Schubert   *Andante* from *Quartet
                 in A Minor*
Shelukov   *Scherzo*
Smith   *Our Favorite*

Grade 3 Solo Literature

Akimento   *Melody*
Anderson   *Nocturne*
Butterworth   *Prelude and Scherzo*
Cherubini   *Sonata no.1*
Clerisse   *Chant sans Paroles*
Cohen   *Legend of the Hills*
Criswell   *Four Interludes*
de Lamartier   *Ballade*
Duck   *The Silver Huntress*
Flegier   *Le Cor*
Gliere   *Intermezzo*
Martini   *Plaisir d'Amour*
Mascagni   *Siciliana*
Mendelssohn   *Romance sans Paroles*
Mozart   *Rondo*, from *Concerto no. 1*
Mozart   *Rondo*, from *Concerto no.3*
Pergolesi   *Sicilienne*
Saint-Saëns   *Romance*
Scriabin   *Romance*
Strauss, F.   *Nocturne*

Grade 4 Solo Literature

Abbot   *Alla Caccia*
Anderson   *March in Canon*
Bach, C. P. E.   *Lament*

Bach, J. S.   *Siciliano*
Cohen   *Fantasy in F Major*
Cooke   *Rondo in B-flat*
Cortese   *Sonata per Corno e Pianoforte*
de Lamartier   *Poème*
Effinger   *Rondino*
Francaix   *Canon in Octave*
Glazunov   *Reverie*
Glière   *Nocturne*
James   *Windmills*
Kauder   *Sonata no.2*
Koetsier   *Romanza*
Mozart   *Concerto no.1*
Poot   *Légende*
Schmid   *Im Tiefsten Walde, op. 24, no.4*
Stevens   *Four Short Pieces*
Tomasi   *Chant Corse*
Weigel   *Maine Sketches*

Grade 5 Solo Literature

Beethoven   *Sonata for Horn and Piano*
Bernstein   *Elegy for Mippy*
Beversdorf   *Sonata for Horn and Piano*
Boutry   *Chassacor*
Chabrier   *Larghetto*
Childs   *Racusen*
Childs   *Variations for David*
Dukas   *Villanelle*
Faust   *Prelude for Horn*
Hartley   *Sonorities II*
Heiden   *Sonata for Horn and Piano*
Hindemith   *Sonata for Alto Horn and Piano*
Hindemith   *Sonata for Horn and Piano*
Koetsier   *Sonatina*
Larsson   *Concertino*
Mozart   *Concerti nos. 2, 3, and 4*
Persichetti   *Parable*
Saint-Saëns   *Morceau de Concert*
Strauss, F.   *Concerto op. 8*
Strauss, F.   *Theme and Variations*
Strauss, R   *Concerto in E-flat, opus II*
Tomasi   *Danse Profane*
Vinter   *Hunter's Moon*

Grade 6 Solo Literature

Adler   *Sonata for Horn and Piano*
Barboteu   *Five Pieces*
Bassett   *Sonata for Horn and Piano*
Bozza   *En Forêt*

Bresgen	*Konzert für Horn*		Jacob	*Concerto*
Buyanovsky	*Pieces for Solo Horn*		Musgrave	*Music for Horn*
Donato	*Sonata*		Persichetti	*Parable*
Dubois	*Concerto*		Rosetti	*Concerto*
Francaix	*Divertimento*		Schreiter	*Sonatine*
Glière	*Concerto*		Stevens	*Sonata*
Haydn	*Concerti nos. 1 and 2*		Strauss, R.	*Concerto no. 2*
Heiden	*Concerto*		Turok	*Sonata*
Heiden	*Sonata*		Wilder	*Sonatas nos. 1 and 2*
Hermanson	*Alarme*			

Selected Discography

American Horn Quartet
   In Autumn, Studio Art Classic AHQ 1295
American Horn Quartet
   American Horn Quartet, ebs records ebs 6008
American Horn Quartet
   The Well-Tempered Horn, ebs 6050
Baumann, Hermann
   Glière Horn Concerto, Philips/BMG D101219
Brain, Dennis
   Mozart Horn Concertos, EMI 55087
Brain, Dennis
   Richard Strauss and Hindemith,
   EMI CDC-7 47834 2

Cerminaro, John
   John Cerminaro, Horn, Crystal Records CD676
Damm, Peter
   Romantic Horn Concertos, Berlin
   Classics 0093242BC
The Horn Club of Los Angeles
   HORNS!, EMI CDM 7 63764 2
Todd, Richard
   Rickter Scale, GM Recordings
   GM 3015CD
Varner, Tom
   Tom Varner, Jazz French Horn, Soul
   Note 121176-2

Selected Bibliography

Bruchle, Bernard. *Horn Bibliographie, Vols. I and II,* Wilhelmshaven: Heinrich Shofen Verlag, 1970.

Farkas, Philip. *The Art of French Horn Playing,* Chicago: Summy-Birchard, 1962.

———. *The Art of Brass Playing,* Rochester, NY: Wind Music, 1962.

———. *The Art of Musicianship,* Miami: Summy-Birchard, 1976.

Hill, Douglas. *Collected Thoughts on Teaching and Learning, Creativity, and Horn Performance,* Miami: Warner Bros., 2001.

Hill, Douglas. *Extended Techniques for the Horn: A Practical Handbook for Students, Performers, and Composers,* Miami: Warner Bros., 1996.

Morley-Pegge, R. *The French Horn,* London: Ernest Benn, 1960.

Tuckwell, Barry. *The Horn,* London: McDonald & Co., 1983.

Wekre, Froydis. *Thoughts on Playing the Horn Well,* Self-published ISBN 82-993244-0-8, 1994.

Harmonic Series, F Horn

Harmonic Series, B-flat Horn

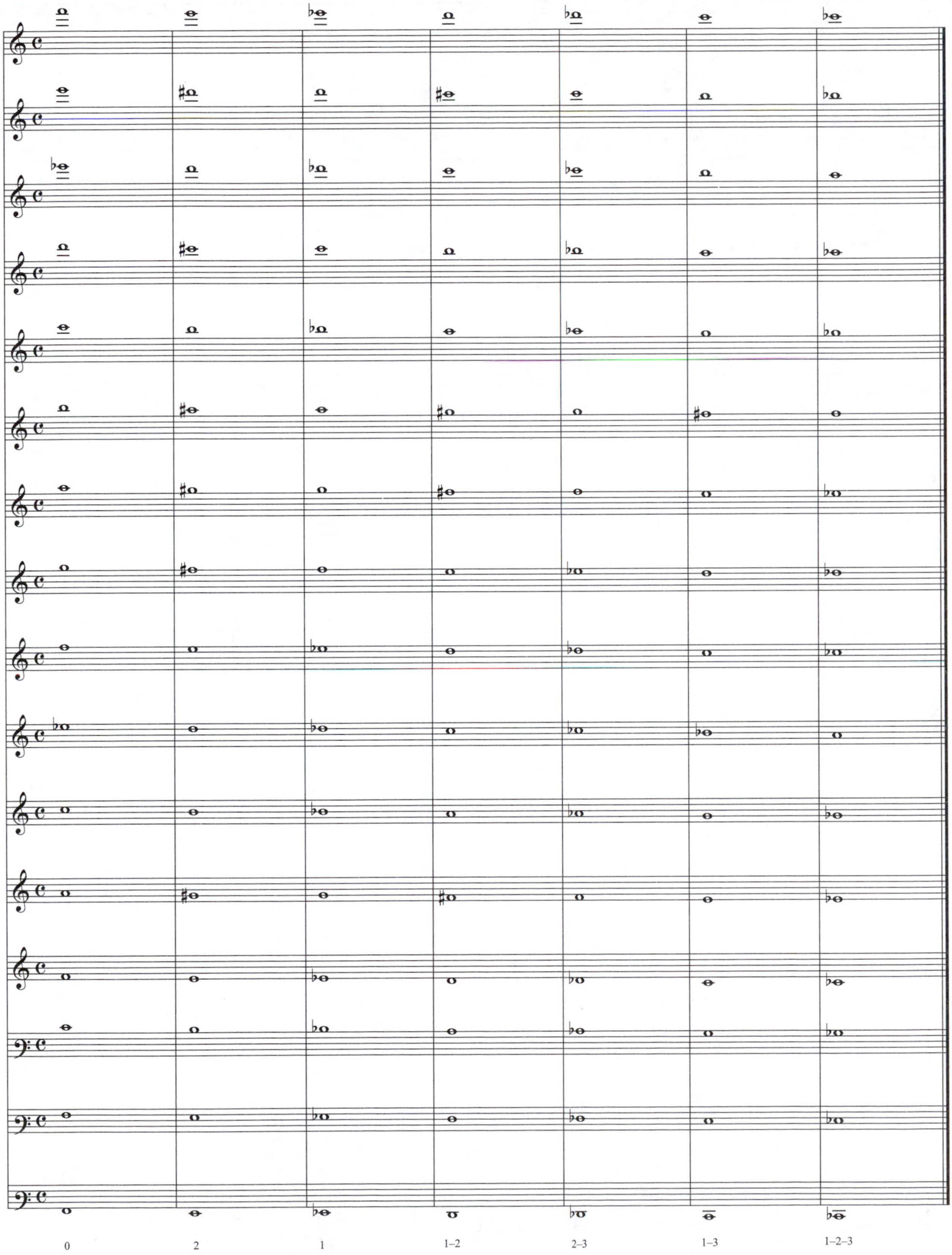

Standard Fingerings, F/B-flat Double Horn

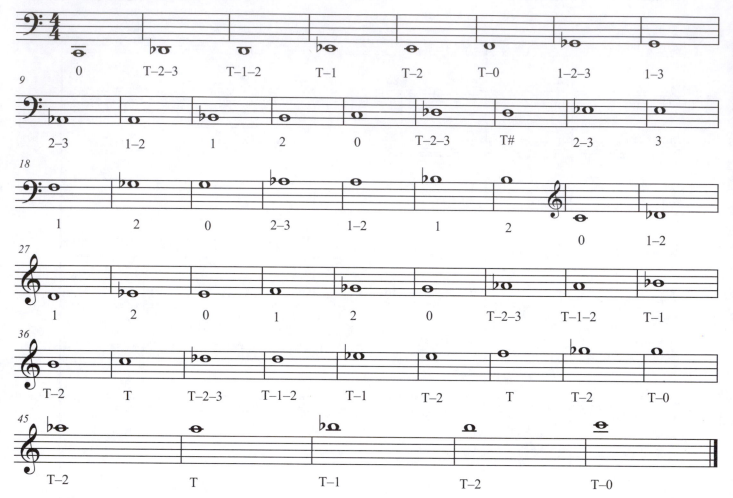

The Trombone

The Tenor Trombone

The tenor trombone is the basic instrument of the trombone family. It is the instrument most often associated with the word trombone and is the instrument of choice for beginners, most students, and most professionals. Like the trumpet, it is a cylindrical brass instrument. In its shortest configuration, the tenor trombone is approximately 9 feet long; it is pitched in B-flat, exactly one octave below the trumpet and a perfect fourth above the horn in F. The trombone is equipped with a cup-shaped mouthpiece.

Tenor trombones tend to vary in overall size much more often than trumpets or horns do. The bell diameters vary from approximately 6 inches to 8.5 inches. Bore diameters of tenor trombones also vary from approximately 0.480 inch to 0.547 inch. These differences provide the wide range of tonal colors required by the diverse musical settings in which trombones are often found.

The most distinctive characteristic of the trombone is the manner in which the length of the instrument is altered to obtain different pitches. Unlike the other brasses, which use a system of valves to engage various lengths of tubing, the trombone is equipped with a telescoping double slide to physically lengthen and shorten the instrument. This slide affords the trained trombonist the opportunity for perfect intonation. Likewise, in the hands of the untrained or the unconcerned, the infinite number of positions possible sometimes produces less than desirable results.

Figure 8–1 illustrates parts of the trombone.

Other Instruments of the Trombone Family

Bass Trombone

From the time of the Renaissance, trombones have been used in families, or *consorts*. A consort is an ensemble of similar instruments pitched from high to

Figure 8–1   Parts of the Trombone

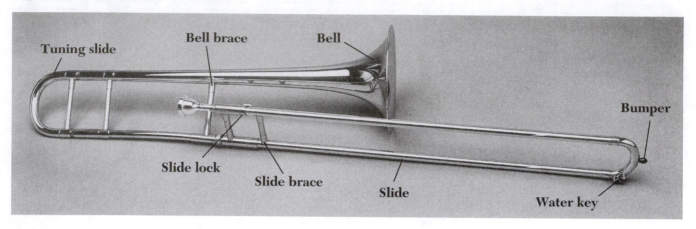

low, coinciding with vocal ranges. This tradition continues today with the use of the bass trombone. Originally, this instrument looked very much like a tenor trombone but with much more length.

Bass trombones are pitched in F, E-flat, or sometimes G below the B-flat tenor. The extreme lengths produced by an extended slide led to the development of the modern bass trombone. This instrument is actually a very large B-flat tenor trombone. The bell of the bass trombone is much larger than the standard tenor bell and ranges from 9.5 to 11.5 inches in diameter. The bore of the bass trombone is generally 0.562 inch, and mouthpieces are comparably larger than those used with the tenor trombone. These alterations darken the timbre of the bass trombone and aid the instrument in producing low pitches. Most bass trombones are also equipped with one or two valves that are used to augment the standard range of the B-flat instrument.

Unlike the bass clarinet, various saxophones, the contrabassoon, and other instruments belonging to a "family," the bass trombone usually is not considered a doubling instrument for a tenor trombonist. The nature of the instrument and its range, timbre, and specific literature demand a specialist.

Alto Trombone

The highest-pitched member of the trombone consort has historically been the alto trombone. This instrument, usually pitched in E-flat, sounds a perfect fourth above the tenor trombone. The bore, bell, and mouthpiece are comparably smaller; consequently, the instrument produces a lighter sound. With the exception of a short period in the early twentieth century, the alto trombone has been used throughout most musical eras. New orchestral, solo, and ensemble literature is being scored with an alto trombone. Because of its shortened positions and high tessitura, it is an instrument best left for the advanced player.

Valve Trombone

The valve trombone is an instrument that is shaped like a slide trombone but which, as the name implies, does not use a slide to change pitches. A set of three valves and corresponding tubing are used in place of the slide. This instrument is used most often by euphonium, baritone, or tuba players in settings where the range or timbre of their usual instruments might not be suitable (for example, in a jazz band or in an ensemble with other trombones). The valve trombone has one major drawback. Unlike most valved brasses, the valve trombone has no means of adjusting the intonation problems inherent in valves. For this reason, its use should be considered carefully.

Figure 8–2 shows some instruments related to the tenor trombone.

Figure 8–2   Related Instruments

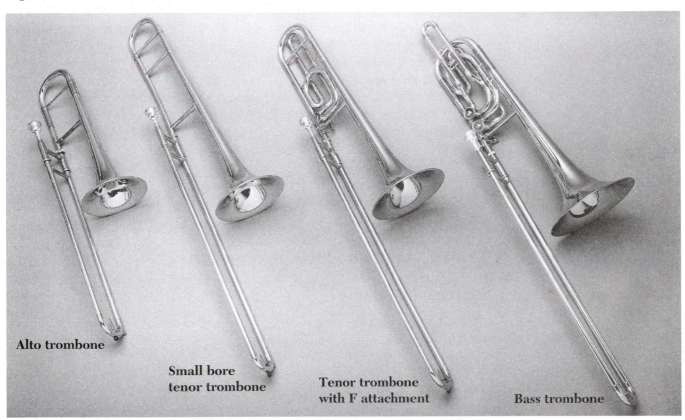

Alto trombone

Small bore tenor trombone

Tenor trombone with F attachment

Bass trombone

Student Qualifications

It is not usually a good idea to start a student on trombone before the fourth or fifth grade. The instrument is somewhat unwieldy even at age 10 or 11. The student should be equipped with normal physical formations—with regard to lips, teeth, jaw, and lungs, for example. It is often thought that long arms are a necessity for playing the trombone. This is not necessarily true and should not be a consideration for the potential trombonist. Most beginning trombonists cannot reach the outer positions.

Of special importance is the ability to match pitches or to sing a melody in tune. Using the slide to change notes demands that the student be able to predict pitches and to discern when pitches do not match.

Assembling the Trombone

The trombone is the only brass instrument that requires some assembly. It is crucial to teach the beginning student the importance of a slow, careful assembly procedure to ensure proper functioning of the instrument. Students should learn the following assembly procedure:

1. Place the unopened case carefully on a chair or the floor with the bell to the left. A trombone case opened on a small student's lap proves very awkward.
2. Open the case and observe how the parts are laid out. They must go back into the case exactly the same way.
3. Unfasten all snaps or other holders.
4. Take the bell section in the left hand. Point the bell toward the floor with the receiver to the right.
5. Take out the slide section with the right hand holding both braces. The "U" should be down.
6. Insert the longer side of the slide section into the bell receiver.
7. Create an angle slightly less than 90 degrees—a moderate "V" between the bell and slide sections.
8. Care should be taken not to bang the slide into the bell.
9. Tighten the bell lock.
10. Insert the mouthpiece into the slide section.
11. Give special attention to the slide at all times to avoid dents.

Proper Hand and Holding Positions

Left-hand Position

The left hand holds the entire weight of the instrument (see Figure 8–3). Consequently, it is very important to develop a proper, yet comfortable, holding position.

Figure 8–3   Left-hand Position

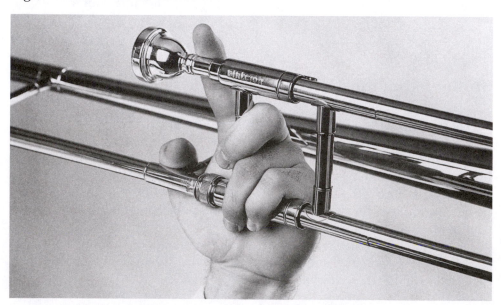

1. Place the thumb around the bell brace. It is not necessary for the bell brace to end up deep in the "V" created by the thumb and index finger. Some trombonists find it more comfortable to place the thumb underneath the neck tube.
2. Extend the index finger comfortably up to the mouthpiece.
3. Wrap the other three fingers comfortably around the stationary slide brace.
4. Maintain a comfortable and relaxed position, and allow for rest breaks. The trombone is a very heavy instrument. Both professionals and students will experience fatigue if rest is not allowed in rehearsals and practice sessions.

Right-hand Position

The right hand moves the slide. None of the instrument's weight should be allowed to shift to the right hand. With the weight in the right hand, the instrument will move too much or the player may develop embouchure problems.

1. Hold the slide brace comfortably with the thumb and the index and middle fingers. Each player will find a natural position.
2. The hand angle should be similar to a salute. This position allows for the natural hinge of the wrist to be relaxed and engaged as necessary.
3. No finger should touch the lower tube of the slide. If this happens, it means that some weight of the instrument is being supported with the right hand.

Figure 8–4 shows the right-hand position on the trombone.

Posture

Proper posture is important for correct breathing, good tone production, and sound projection. The player should be comfortably upright whether sitting or

Figure 8–4   Right-hand Position

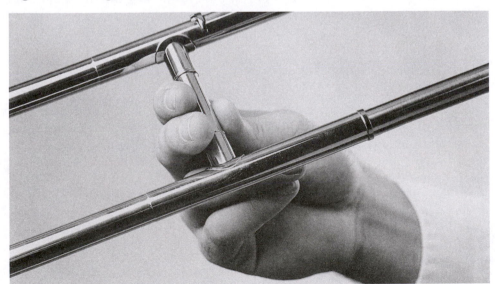

Figure 8–5   Sitting Position

standing. When standing, the player should place equal weight on both feet and hold the head up as if looking toward the horizon. When sitting, the player should maintain the same erect posture with the upper body. Chairs with seats that angle back tend to restrict the breathing process and should be avoided. Whether sitting or standing, it is important for the player to bring the instrument to the lips without changing the upright posture or creating undue tension. The player should never tilt the head or crane the neck to reach for the instrument. With much of the weight on the left side of the body, this tendency is common among young players.

Figure 8–5 shows the correct sitting position for playing the trombone, and Figure 8–6 shows the correct standing position.

Embouchure Specifics

Most trombonists are in agreement that the mouthpiece should be centered on the lips from left to right. Some individual variation is always acceptable as long as extremes are avoided. There is much less agreement among trombonists regarding the placement of the mouthpiece vertically on the lips. Many great players play the trombone with a "high" setting—two-thirds upper lip, one-third lower lip—which is similar to the horn setting. Others do very well with a "low" setting—one-third upper lip, two-thirds lower. Others place half of the mouthpiece on each lip. Because of the size of the mouthpiece, it is advisable to start with the mouthpiece approximately half on each lip and allow each player to find the best setting.

Figure 8–6   Standing Position

Forming the Trombone Embouchure

The lip formation for a correct trombone embouchure can be described as follows:

1. The lips are together.
2. The jaw drops comfortably down and slightly out, without contortion or tense extension.
3. The chin is flat.
4. The muscles around the lips form a slight cushion for the mouthpiece rim.
5. The corners are firm—not pulled back into a smile.
6. Excessive mouthpiece pressure, especially on the upper lip, should be avoided at all times.

This embouchure formation allows the lips to vibrate with maximum efficiency. At the same time, it will create the correct shape inside the mouth. The oral cavity should be very large, open, and relaxed. The tongue also should be low and relaxed. This openness allows the greatest amount of control in the manipulation of the airstream and consequently produces the characteristic trombone sound.

Proper embouchure development and breathing habits are perhaps the most important elements for the beginning trombonist. Technique, tone quality, and

Figure 8–7   Trombone Embouchure

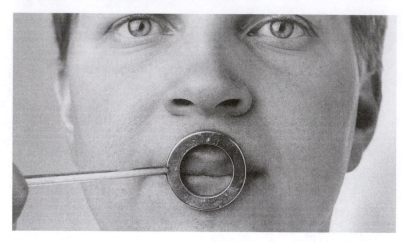

true intonation are all a direct result of a properly formed embouchure. The student who combines correct embouchure with the proper manipulation of the airstream exhibits great improvement over time.

The correct trombone embouchure is illustrated in Figure 8–7.

Strengthening the Embouchure

Techniques to aid in embouchure development are often practiced away from the instrument. Exercising the embouchure alone is an extremely efficient way to develop the embouchure. The following exercises should be used in moderation, as a complement to practicing the instrument itself, which is necessary for working on more musical sounds.

1. *Lip buzzing.* Sometimes called "freebuzzing," forming the lips into the correct shape and attempting to vibrate them without mouthpiece or instrument is an excellent method for achieving the necessary strength to sustain a tone. Monitor lip buzzing constantly to ensure a correct approach. When a tone can be sustained, encourage the student to "bend" the pitch slightly in each direction. As the embouchure develops further, the student should try to match pitches and to sound scale patterns and easy tunes.
2. *Mouthpiece buzzing.* This practice technique, similar to lip buzzing, is used by most brass players to aid embouchure development, to exercise proper use of air, and to work on a clear, resonant tone. Additionally, mouthpiece buzzing requires that the student produce musical sounds without the aid of the instrument—a skill required for the trombonist. Give special care to ensure proper formation of the lips, shape of the oral cavity, and use of air.

Embouchure Problems

Many of the problems outlined in Chapter 3 are common on the trombone. Of these, the most common are excessive mouthpiece pressure and the resultant "puffy" cheeks. Refer to Chapter 3 for solutions to these problems.

Articulation

Basic Articulation

The placement of the tongue when articulating on the trombone is slightly more forward than a normal speaking placement, with the tip generally touching the back of the upper teeth. The rest of the tongue should be as relaxed as possible. The motion of articulation is best described as an up-and-down motion rather than back and forth. The syllables used in basic articulation for the trombone are those that allow the jaw to be down, creating a large oral cavity: "toe" or "taw." Refer to exercises 9C, 9D, 10A, 10B, 11B, 13A, 13C, 15B, 16B, 21D, and 22C for practice using single tonguing.

Multiple Tonguing

Both double and triple tonguing are possible on the trombone. The development of these articulations has been described in the preceding chapters and is much the same for the trombone. Special problems concerning multiple tonguing and slide technique will be addressed later in this chapter. Refer to exercises 40D, 46D, 48B, 49C, 49D, 50C, 51C, 53D for practice using double tonguing. Refer to exercises 38D, 50D, 51B, 52C, and 53C for practice using triple tonguing.

Legato Style

The primary consideration when playing in a smooth or legato style is to sustain pitches. When one note is played its full value and the next note is started immediately and sustained for its full value, the change between notes sounds smooth. This is accomplished, primarily, by a continuous flow of air. These lyric settings require a softer sound at the beginning of the note. Trombonists use the syllables "doe," "daw," "noe," or "nah." Even with continuous airflow and when a soft articulation is used to perform a legato passage, a glissando (normally avoided) sometimes occurs. To cope with this problem, the trombonist must develop an approach to playing legato that is unique to the brasses.

To play legato on the trombone

1. The trombonist must maintain a continuous airflow. This is fundamental to playing legato on any wind instrument. If the air stops, the sound stops, and the overall effect is not smooth.
2. The slide must move very quickly between notes, exactly in rhythm, and it must stop on each note. If the slide is moved before a note is finished, a glissando occurs. It is also necessary to move the slide smoothly, without jerking it violently, so that the musical line can be maintained.
3. A light articulation (usually with a *d* or *n*) must be used. This must be coordinated exactly with the motion of the slide.
4. It is not always necessary to use the soft articulation when changing partials. There is some disagreement among trombonists about this; many use these "natural slurs" whenever possible, whereas others use predominantly legato (articulated) slurs to maintain consistency of sound.

Figure 8–8   Legato Exercises

Play in all major and minor keys.

Play in all positions.

You should keep in mind that the overall sound desired is a smooth, lyric, singing quality. If the sound produced does not sound smooth, most likely the trombonist is not sustaining pitches with air. If there are smears before or after the notes, the slide probably needs to move more quickly and more in rhythm. . A very common problem found in student trombonists (and their teachers) is an unnecessary emphasis on the soft tongue stroke— "legato tonguing." Fine legato performance occurs for trombonists when all three elements—continuous air, slide technique, and soft tongue—are engaged in perfect balance. Refer to exercises 23D, 25D, 33B, 35A, 36D, 42C, 44D, 48A, 50A, and 51D for slurring exercises. Figure 8–8 demonstrates legato exercises for the trombone.

Breath Control

Inhalation

To produce a tone on the trombone, a full, deep breath should be taken using an open vowel ("oh," "ah"). Many teachers suggest taking the breath from the corners of the mouth. Generally, this does not work well on low brass instruments. Stretching the lips horizontally destroys the correct embouchure formation, tightens the lips, and does not allow for the openness necessary for taking in the large quantities of air used in low brass playing. Teach the student to allow the lower lip to drop slightly so that the breath can be taken in through an open mouth. Special care should be taken to make sure that the lower lip returns to its proper place for the next articulation.

Exhalation

The full, deep inhalation is followed immediately by a relaxed yet energetic flow of air blown out. If the embouchure is formed correctly, there will be no obstruction to the flow of air until it reaches the lips. Tension should be avoided at all points in the breathing mechanism. Any mention of "putting muscles to work" adds unnecessary tension. Teach the student simply to blow and to feel as though the air were flowing from the lower part of the lungs first.

Beginning the First Tone

The first note played by a beginner is necessarily a combination of all the information given so far. The student must breathe in, form an embouchure, articulate and blow out, and buzz the lips. One can only imagine the confusion of a beginner confronted with the detail presented thus far. A simplified procedure is suggested:

1. Begin with a simple discussion of deep breathing and free, relaxed blowing.
2. A simple description of embouchure formation might be, "Get ready to say 'Moe.'" Make sure that the lips are together.
3. Breathe deeply and buzz the lips alone, with no articulation.
4. Buzz the mouthpiece on any pitch.
5. Sustain any pitch on the mouthpiece.
6. Replace the mouthpiece and resonate the instrument on any pitch in first position without articulation.
7. Add an articulation: "Start the air by saying 'Toe.'" (Make sure that the lips start together and are blown apart.)

The Overtone Series of the Trombone

Knowledge of the intonation tendencies of the natural overtone series is also important for the trombonist. Figure 8–9 shows the tendencies for the first eight partials of the trombone in first position. These tendencies continue through all seven positions and become even more noticeable as the slide is extended. Consult the overtone series chart at the end of this chapter.

Figure 8–9   Overtone Series of the Trombone, 1st Position

Intonation Tendencies

As with any brass instrument, the proportion of added tubing needed to lower pitches on the trombone reflects the same acoustic principles stated earlier. The inherent intonation problems of valves used in combination are not a problem on the trombone. It is possible, and correct, to make each position slightly longer as the slide is extended. This provides the trombone with the inherent capability of playing perfectly in tune. However, the infinite number of out-of-tune slide placements creates many problems, especially for the beginning trombonist.

Obviously, some consistency is required to limit these incorrect placements. To play in tune on the trombone, the student must be taught a few fundamentals:

1. *Centered blowing.* Do not teach the student to adjust the pitch of a note by firming or relaxing the embouchure. "Lipping" notes adds more inconsistency; blowing centered is dependable. Any pitch adjustments should be made with the slide.
2. *Listen ahead.* Encourage the student to listen for the next note. With an expected pitch in the ear, the player hears discrepancies between that pitch

and the actual sounding pitch. The student should be encouraged to play and sing many well-known tunes and scales to practice this. Mouthpiece buzzing is also an excellent tool to develop this internalized music making.

3. *Adjust the slide up or down as necessary when discrepancies are heard.* This is usually a very natural ability. Muscle memory, a fundamental requisite for playing in tune, is then reinforced. The slide, given time and practice, ends up very close to the correct place so that fine adjustments can be made.

Never teach the student to touch the bell with a finger to help find a position. This "fixes" the length of tubing much as a valve does, and does not allow for fine-tuning adjustments. Technique can also be adversely affected. The intonation of a beginning trombonist can be gruesome. Undeveloped embouchures and evolving breathing habits combined with an awkward slide technique can create some bizarre sounds. The conscientious teacher is aware of this and, using the guidelines of this chapter, gently monitors the intonation of the trombone section at all times.

Ranges

Expanding the range, both high and low, is of universal concern to brass players. To sound a higher note, the player must vibrate the lips faster; to play a lower note, slower vibration is required. Such often-suggested procedures as "focus the embouchure" and "diminish the aperture size" for high notes, and "increase the air supply" and "open the aperture" for low notes, are methods for producing the proper speed of vibration. Figure 8–10 shows recommended register guidelines for teaching the trombone.

Range expansion should always be accomplished slowly and carefully without excessive stress or tension. Consistent tone quality is the determinant for continued range expansion.

Figure 8–10   Suggested Register Guidelines for the Trombone

Beginning   Intermediate   Advanced

Warm-up and Practice Techniques

In addition to preparation of music for performance, the trombonist should have a daily practice routine. This should consist of a short warm-up period in which the student buzzes the mouthpiece and plays easy scales, patterns, and lip slurs in a moderate range. Careful practice of fundamental techniques follows the warm-up and should constitute one-fourth to one-half of the total practice time. Included in this daily routine should be exercises such as those shown in Figure 8–11:

Figure 8–11   Warm-up Exercises

Long Tones

Long Slurs

Tonguing

These are only examples of the types of exercises that should be practiced. Expansion of range, dynamic control, and other aspects of technique can be accomplished by extending these basic studies as control allows.

Specific Techniques for the Trombone

Slide Technique

If you are not a trombonist, you may feel a certain apprehension about teaching the use of the slide to change pitches. If you take the time to learn about the slide and its difficulties and advantages, the anxiety of teaching it to others will be alleviated.

Beginning trombonists may need more time than their valve-playing friends to become accustomed to their instrument. The motion used to operate the slide is not complex and should be taught in the simplest, most natural way possible: Generally, if the right-hand position, as described earlier, is applied with a relaxed grip, the proper slide motion is a natural result. To move the slide out, the right thumb tends to initiate the motion, and the knuckle of the right index finger tends to lead or direct the motion. A natural braking action is employed when it is time to stop. When the slide is moved in, the roles of the fingers and thumb are reversed. The wrist should be relaxed, but in control, at all times.

Trombonists are called upon to perform in all tempi. Generally speaking, when the notes are long or move slowly, teach the trombonist to move the slide in rhythm; when the notes change, the slide moves quickly. There is a tendency instead, especially in younger players, to stop the sound of a note so that the slide can be moved to the next note without a glissando. Coordinating the slide in motion with the articulation and air creates the proper sounds and should be monitored constantly.

As tempi and/or rhythms quicken, it becomes necessary to keep the slide in motion and articulate the notes (with single or multiple tonguing) as the slide goes by. Generally, in these situations, the trombonist attempts to keep the slide moving in one direction as long as possible by using alternative positions. This is an advanced technique and should be taught only when the student has a good grasp of the fundamentals. As with any learned physical motion, visual example and the student's repeated experiences often prove to be the best teaching technique.

Glissando

The most distinctive special effect that can be played on the trombone is the glissando. Sliding from one note to another without articulations is technically known as "portamento," but through common usage, the term "glissando" is used and is notated most often for this sound in trombone parts. The trombone is singular among the brasses in its ability to accomplish this effect, often to most everyone's amusement. Glissandi must be scored within a partial, making the tritone the widest interval possible. Figure 8–12 illustrates the glissando on the trombone.

A true "piano" or "harp" glissando, moving rapidly through scalelike passages, can also be performed on the trombone. A combination of ascending lip slurs with outward motion of the slide (or descending slurs with inward motion) can create a true glissando. This is sometimes referred to as "across-the-grain" slurring.

Figure 8–12   Glissando

Vibrato

Three types of vibrato are available to the trombonist. The lip or jaw vibrato is probably the most often used and is effective. Pulsations in intensity are added to the tone by slight fluctuations in the lips or jaw, as if saying "woe-woe-woe."

A back-and-forth motion of the slide will create a pitch-change vibrato. This slide vibrato is used cautiously in "classical" settings, with an oscillation between the actual pitch and slightly below. Slide vibrato is used more often in commercial and jazz settings, in which it moves both lower and higher than the actual pitch to give the characteristic quality to the sound.

The third type of vibrato involves pulsations in the airstream, as if pronouncing "ho-ho-ho." This intensity vibrato is very difficult to learn and is best left to the advanced player in consultation with a private teacher.

Clefs

The literature for trombone often calls for a variety of clefs:

1. Bass clef is the basic clef learned first by trombonists.
2. Tenor clef places middle C on the fourth line of the staff. This is used in all types of advanced literature and should be introduced in high school.
3. Alto clef places middle C on the middle line. This clef is used in advanced solo and orchestral literature. It should be introduced when tenor clef is well learned.
4. Treble clef is sometimes used in very advanced literature. When it is, the notes sound as written.
5. B-flat treble clef is used when a trombonist is called on to play a treble clef baritone, tenor saxophone, trumpet, or clarinet part. Also, literature coming from the British brass band tradition may be notated in B-flat treble clef. The trombonist can mentally add two flats (subtract two sharps) and read the music in tenor clef. The notes will sound down a major ninth from written pitch.

Lip Trills

Lip trills are created by rapid back-and-forth lip slurs between adjacent notes in the overtone series. Consequently, lip trills work best in the upper register, where the notes are closer together. Refer to Chapter 7, "The horn," for specific instruction on the production of lip trills.

Multiphonics

Multiphonics are created by playing a note while simultaneously allowing the air to vibrate the vocal chords on another pitch. This works especially well on the lower brasses because of the range of the average voice; it is easier to sing above the played note. When multiphonics are performed correctly with certain pitches, complete triads sound as a result of summation and difference tones.

Choosing a Trombone and Other Equipment

Recommended Trombones

Beginner Trombones

Most manufacturers produce a line of trombones designed for the beginning student. These are always small-bore instruments (about 0.500 inch) and are built with attention directed to sturdiness rather than fine craftsmanship. These instruments are ideal for a beginning student who is learning how to handle the trombone. In selecting an instrument, it is crucial for the slide to work well when not lubricated. Any dents, flat spots, or misalignment cannot be corrected by lubrication and will be detrimental to the progress of the student. Beginners should never purchase trombones equipped with an F attachment. The extra cost is unnecessary, and the added weight can cause problems in posture, tone production, and ease of playing.

Recommended Beginner Trombones

> Yamaha YSL-354
> Bach TB 200
> Bundy 1523
> Conn USA
> Getzen 351

Professional-Quality Small-Bore Trombones

Small-bore instruments are also produced with professional-quality materials and workmanship. These instruments are used most often by the advanced player in commercial or jazz settings. The smaller bore and compatibly smaller mouthpiece produce a brighter, lighter sound that is more characteristic of jazz. Generally, the advanced student and the professional will own both this "little horn" and a "big horn."

Recommended Professional-Quality Small-Bore Trombones

> Yamaha YSL-691, YSL-695
> Bach 12, 16, 16M
> Conn 6H, 100H
> King 2102, 2103

Medium-Bore Trombones

Most instrument makers also produce a medium-bore trombone (0.525 inch). This instrument is sometimes used by the advanced high school student as a convenient step to the large-bore trombone. It is best to solicit the opinion of a private teacher or professional before purchasing this instrument.

Recommended Medium-Bore Trombones

(Model number in parentheses has an F attachment.)

> Bach 36 (36B)
> Yamaha YSL-683 (684), 645 (646)
> Conn 7H (78H)

Large-Bore Trombones

The large-bore trombone (0.547 inch) is the instrument of choice for the advanced student and the professional in most settings other than jazz. Large-bore trombones are used in orchestral, band, solo, and chamber ensemble playing situations and are often equipped with the F attachment.

Recommended Large-Bore Trombones

(Model number in parentheses has an F attachment.)

> Bach 42 (42B)
> YSL-8820 Xeno
> Conn 8H (88H)
> Benge 190 (190F)

Recommended Bass Trombones

Bass trombones, as described earlier in this chapter, are actually very large versions of the tenor trombone. The larger bore (0.562 inch) and bell (9.5 to 11.5 inches) provide easier access to lower notes and render a darker, deeper tone quality. Bass trombones are always equipped with an F attachment, and most include a second valve tuned to E, E-flat, or D to provide the complete chromatic range below E. Bass trombones complete a trombone section, and at least one should be owned by high schools and colleges. Players who choose to play the bass trombone most often become specialists on it because of its particular playing characteristics and sound.

The following are some recommended bass trombones. The model given in parentheses is equipped with a second valve.

> Bach 50B, (50B2) 50B3
> Yamaha YBL-613, YBL 622
> Conn 110H, (112H)
> Getzen 1052FD
> Getzen 1062FD

Custom trombones and valves are available. Because of their high cost and specific function, these are best used mainly by the professional. Many custom, high-end professional models of trombones are available and are quite popular. Makers such as Edwards, Shires, Thein, and others are making very high-quality large tenors, small tenors, bass trombones, and alto trombones. These are generally quite expensive and are best left to the professional or for students in consultation with their private teacher. Several of the better-known factory instruments now offer convertible/custom options as well. An explosion of innovation in valve design has led to several alternatives to the standard rotary valve (see F-attachment below). The Thayer axial-flow valve, Hagemann valve, Greenhoe valve, Lindberg valve, Shires rotary valve, and others are available and in use by trombonists. Each offers a unique design, usually a hefty price tag, and generally improved performance. Again, consultation with a private teacher or local professional is advised.

Mouthpieces

Trombone mouthpieces come in two distinct shank sizes. The small-shank mouthpiece is designed to fit the small- and medium-bore trombones. The large-shank mouthpiece is designed to fit large-bore and bass trombones. Adapters are available for a small shank to fit a large instrument, but these are not recommended.

When selecting a mouthpiece, it is always best to solicit the opinion of a private teacher or professional. Generally, avoid extremes. The cup should not be too shallow or too deep; the rim should be of average width with a diameter that feels good to the individual player. The mouthpiece should also be matched to the instrument to produce the desired tone quality.

Recommended Mouthpieces

Beginner

(These should be used for a year or two at most.)

> Bach 12C, 11C, 7C
> Schilke 47, 48, 49

Intermediate

> Bach 7C, 6 1/2 AL
> Schilke 50

Advanced

> Bach 6½AL, 5G, 5GS
> Schilke 51, 51B, 51D, 52D, 52E2

Bass Trombone

> Bach 1G, 1½G, 2G, 3G
> Schilke 57, 58, 59, 60

These recommendations represent a small number of the brands and sizes available. Many other fine mouthpieces are not listed, any of which could be the best mouthpiece for a given trombonist.

The F Attachment

The F attachment is an extra set of tubing that can be added to the open instrument by use of a left-thumb rotary valve. The attachment has three main purposes:

1. *Extension of the low range* (see Figure 8–13). When the valve is engaged, the trombonist has the F overtone series in first position, the E series in a slightly lowered second position, and E-flat in a lowered third position. These chromatics continue through the C overtone series in flat seventh position. Low B natural is acoustically impossible unless the F attachment tuning slide is extended.

Figure 8–13

v1   vb2   vb3   v#5   v6   vb7

Figure 8–14

```
1    6    1    6    1    6    1    6
1    v1   1    v1   1    v1   1    v1
```

Figure 8–15

2. *Technique* (see Figure 8–14). Some technically awkward slide positioning can be made easier with the F attachment.
3. *Special effects* (see Figure 8–15). Some trills and other effects can be executed with the F attachment.

The F attachment is rarely used above the C in bass clef. Tune it so that the same C is perfectly in tune when playing the B-flat major scale.

Never recommend the purchase of a trombone with F attachment for beginners. The added weight always causes problems, and the attachment can become a poor substitute for learning the outer positions.

Mutes

A full complement of mutes is available for the trombone. The straight mute is the most often required. Metal is preferred; plastic and fiber are also used.

Recommended Straight Mutes

> Tom Crown
> Jo-Ral
> Denis Wick

Cup mutes are available, made of metal or fiber. Fiber mutes provide a very good sound but are often deficient in producing low pitches. Metal cup mutes produce good sounds throughout the entire range.

Recommended Cup Mutes

> Humes and Berg (fiber)
> Denis Wick (metal, adjustable cup)
> Jo-Ral (metal, adjustable cup)
> TrumCor

Other mutes used by trombonists include the Harmon (Wick, Jo-Ral), bucket, plunger, and practice mutes, and hats. Each provides a unique sound as dictated by musical considerations. Miscellaneous equipment used by trombonists include a water bottle to spray the slide, a trombone stand, and a mute bag (most mutes do not fit in the case).

Cleaning and Maintaining the Trombone

Cleaning the Trombone

The trombone should be cleaned periodically, usually four to six times per year. A bathtub or similar large facility should be used because most sinks are not large enough. Damage usually results when cleaning is attempted anywhere but in the tub.

A sample cleaning routine includes these steps:

1. Fill the bathtub with *warm* (*NOT HOT*) water.
2. Disassemble the trombone, removing all slides.
3. Soak all parts.
4. Use a flexible snake to clean the inner parts of the slide.
5. Flush all other parts—bell, tuning slide, and so forth—using the tub faucet.
6. Dry everything, relubricate, and reassemble.

Intermittently, the slide can be cleaned by filling the complete slide section with warm water and working the slide back and forth to dislodge any foreign matter.

Lubricants

A slide that works well is the unending pursuit of most trombonists. One commonly used lubricant is slide oil. This is easy to use and works best for the beginning trombonist. Other methods of slide lubrication described next require the use of a bottle to spray the slide with water. The use of these spray bottles should be considered carefully in a class of young trombonists.

A second method of lubricating the slide uses silicone cream and water. This method is more expensive and more time consuming, but is considered best by many trombonists.

To clean and lubricate the slide, follow these steps:

1. With the instrument disassembled, remove the hand slide and set it aside carefully.
2. Wipe off the outer part of the inner slide.
3. Apply a small amount of oil or silicone cream (never both) to the outer part of the inner slide.
4. If using oil, replace the hand slide.
5. If using cream, spread it evenly over the slightly raised tubing at the ends of the inner slide (called "stockings").
6. Spray the inner slide with water.
7. Replace the hand slide and work it back and forth.
8. Reapply water and remove excess cream as needed. (Optional step: Wipe the inner slide again; spread a small amount of silicone *liquid* over the stockings.)
9. Spray with water. Replace the slide.

A third slide lubrication system is marketed under the brand name "Slide-O-Mix." This is a three-bottle system (two of lubricants and one of water) that is clean, easy to use, and the choice of many trombonists.

Even the smallest dent in the slide causes it to operate poorly. This is very discouraging for beginning students and a very real nuisance for advanced players. Slide dents should be repaired as soon as possible to avoid plating wear on the inner slide.

The slide tubes, outer and inner, must be in perfect alignment for the slide to operate efficiently. Bowing is often caused by resting the trombone vertically on the slide. Do not allow the beginner to form this habit.

Tuning slides must also be kept lubricated. Ideally, the lubricant used will allow the slide to move easily and stay where it is placed. Special tuning slide lubricants are produced by many manufacturers.

Cleaners

Trombonists should own a mouthpiece brush that should be run through the mouthpiece daily. A trombone slide snake removes deposits from the long, straight slide sections. Cleaning rods, available for the same purpose, should be wrapped carefully with a lint-free cloth and used to clean the outer slide only. If a cleaning rod is used to clean the inner slides, damage to the acoustically sensitive leadpipe results.

History of the Trombone

The trombone dates its origin to the development and addition of the telescoping double slide to the natural trumpet. At that point, circa 1450, a brass instrument with complete chromatic capability was available. Even though the early trombones had narrower bores and funnel-shaped bells, the manner of changing notes on the trombone has remained virtually unchanged to this day.

Throughout the Renaissance, this instrument (called "sackbut" in England, "posaune" in Germany, and "trombone" in Italy) was used in its various sizes to double voices in choirs, as well as participate in instrumental consorts. This tradition of trombones in combination with voices led to a somewhat lesser role during the Baroque era. Increased emphasis on instrumental music and the predominance of a (usually treble) melodic line relegated trombones almost solely to the opera (for instance, in Gluck) and oratorio (in Handel, for example). In some areas, probably where exceptional trombonists were located, the trombone was used in solo settings as part of trio or quartet sonatas. Composers such as Fux, Biber, Bertali, and Vejvanovsky used the trombone in such settings.

In the Classical period, the trombone continued to be used in the operas, oratorios, and sacred compositions of major composers such as Mozart and Haydn. In addition, soloistic uses continued. Some solo movements are found in divertimenti of Michael Haydn and Leopold Mozart. Complete concerti were composed by Albrechtsberger and Wagenseil.

In the Romantic era, the composers continued using the trombone in vocal settings and soloistically, and the trombone was admitted to the standard orchestral setting (most often attributed to Beethoven's Fifth Symphony). As the nineteenth century progressed, the trombone section (still alto, tenor, and bass) was given important roles in most symphonic output. The symphonies of Schubert, Mendelssohn, Schumann, and Brahms have significant trombone parts.

During the twentieth century, the trombone found its greatest use since the Renaissance. Trombones are used in virtually all settings: symphonic, chamber, solo, popular, and jazz. In contemporary literature the trombone seems to be a favorite of many composers, probably because of its wide range, its potential for timbral variation, and its ability to perform many special effects.

Graded Literature Lists

Method Books, Beginning

Arban/Randal	*Complete Method*
Cimera	*170 Studies*
Cimera	*221 Progressive Studies*
Cimera/Hovey	*Method for Trombone*
Rubank/Long	*Elementary Method*

Method Books, Intermediate

Blume	*36 Studies*
Cimera	*79 Studies*
Ervin	*Range Building on the Trombone*
Fink	*Introducing the F Attachment*
Hering	*40 Études*
Pederson	*Elementary Technical Studies*
Voxman	*Selected Studies*

Method Books, Advanced

Bitsch	*15 Rhythmic Studies*
Boutry	*12 Études*
Bozza	*13 Capriccio Studies*
Couillaud	*30 Modern Studies*
Maenz	*12 Studies*
Maxted	*20 Studies*
Tyrrell	*40 Progressive Studies*
Vernon	*A "Singing" Approach to the Trombone (and other Brass)*

Legato Studies

Bordogni/Rochut	*Melodious Études (three volumes)*
Cimera	*55 Phrasing Studies*
Fink	*Studies in Legato*
Fink	*Introducing Legato*

Clef Studies

Blazevich	*Clef Studies*
Edwards	*Introductory Studies in Tenor and Alto Clef*
Fink	*Introducing Alto Clef*
Fink	*Introducing Tenor Clef*

Kahila	*Advanced Studies*
Sauer	*Clef Studies*

Method Books, Bass Trombone, Beginning

Ostrander	*Method for Bass Trombone*
Roberts/Tanner	*Let's Play Bass Trombone*

Method Books, Bass Trombone, Intermediate

Blume/Fink	*36 Studies*
Gillis	*70 Progressive Studies*
Kopprasch/Fote	*Selected Studies*
Ostrander	*Basic Studies*

Method Books, Bass Trombone, Advanced

Gilllis	*20 Études*
Grigoriev	*24 Studies*
Ostrander	*Shifting Meter Studies*
Raph	*Double-Valve Bass Trombone*
Vernon	*A "Singing" Approach to the Trombone (and other Brass)*

Grade 1 Solo Literature, Tenor Trombone

Buchtel	*Argonaut Waltz*
Buchtel	*At the Ball*
Buchtel	*Beau Brummel*
Buchtel	*Fandango*
Buchtel	*Pied Piper*
Tanner	*Hot Taco*
Tanner	*Soloist Folio*
Tanner	*Wade in the Water*

Grade 2 Solo Literature

Barnes	*Trombone Album*
Buchtel	*Intermezzo*
Buchtel	*Jovial Mood*
Clarke, E.	*Devotion*
Harris	*Sparkles*
Smith	*First Solos*
Smith	*Gaslight*
Vandercook	*Emerald*

Vandercook   *Ruby*
Vandercook   *Turquoise*

Grade 3 Solo Literature

Barnes   *Arioso and Caprice*
Buchtel   *Jupiter*
Burgstahler   *Triumphant Trombone*
Cimera   *Victoria*
Clarke, E.   *Artemis Polka*
Fox   *Andante and March*
Johnson   *Pastel Prairies*
Ostransky   *Two Spanish Dances*
Vandercook   *Garnet*
Vandercook   *Topaz*

Grade 4 Solo Literature

Bakaleinikoff   *Andante Cantabile*
Baker and Hanson   *Songs for the Young Trombonist*
Beach   *Suite*
Cimera   *Betsy Waltz*
Cimera   *Caprice Charmante*
Hasse   *Hasse Suite*
Johnson   *Lyric Interlude*
Pryor   *La Petite Suzanne*
Ropartz   *Andante et Allegro*
Smith   *Solos for Trombone*
Voxman   *Concert and Contest Collection*

Grade 5 Solo Literature

Alary   *Concert Piece*
Barat   *Andante et Allegro*
Blazevich   *Concert Sketch No.5*
David   *Concertino*
Dubois   *Cortege*
Graefe   *Concerto*
Guilmant   *Morceau Symphonique*
Nestico   *Reflective Mood*
Pryor   *Thoughts of Love*
Simons   *Atlantic Zephyr*

Grade 6 Solo Literature

Bloch   *Symphony*
Bozza   *Ballade*
Casterade   *Sonatina*

Chavez   *Concerto*
Creston   *Fantasy*
Ewazen   *Sonata*
Peaslee   *Arrows of Time*
Rouse   *Concerto*
Hindemith   *Sonata*
Imbrie   *Three Sketches*
Jacob   *Concerto*
Serocki   *Sonatina*
Stevens   *Sonata*

Grade 5 Solo Literature, Bass Trombone

Barat   *Introduction and Serenade*
Bartles   *Elegy*
Capuzzi   *Andante and Rondo*
Dedrick   *Lyric Étude*
Dubois   *Si Trombone en Était*
Frescobaldi   *Canzoni*
Garlick   *Sonata*
Hartley   *Arioso*
Hoffman   *The Big Horn*
McCarty   *Sonata*
McKay   *Suite*
Stevens   *Sonatina*
Tcherepnin   *Andante*

Grade 6 Solo Literature, Bass Trombone

Bozza   *Andante et Allegro*
Castérède   *Fantaisie Concertante*
Croley   *Divertissement*
Ewazen   *Concerto*
Gillingham   *Sonata*
Grantham   *Sonata in One Movement*
Koetsier   *Allegro Maestoso*
Levedev   *Concerto in One Movement*
Liptak   *Flaming Angel*
McCarty   *Sonata*
Spillman   *Concerto*
Stevens   *Sonatina*
White   *Tetra Ergon*
Wilder   *Sonata*

Selected Discography

Alessi, Joseph
> *Slide Area,* Summit Records DCD 130
> *New York Legends,* Cala Records CACD0508
> *Trombonastics,* Summit Records DCD 314

Lawrence, Mark
> *Trombonology,* d'Note Classics DND 1012

Lenthe, Carl
> *The Audition Window—Timeless Trombone Tales,* Summit DCD 354

Lindberg, Christian
> *The Virtuoso Trombone,* BIS CD 258
> *Romantic Trombone,* BIS CD 298
> *The Burlesque Trombone,* BIS CD 318
> *American Trombone Concertos,* BIS CD 628
> *American Trombone Concertos,* vol. II, BIS CD788
> *Romantic Trombone Concertos,* BIS CD 378

Lucas, Don
> *Cantabile,* Don Louca, n.d.

Markey, James
> *Offroad,* James Marke, 2003

Mauger, Jacques
> *Concertos for Trombone,* Production Orchestra Symphonique Francais, OSF 49022

Miller, James
> *From Coast to Coast,* All Barks Dog Records

Sauer, Ralph
> *Plays,* Crystal 380

Vining, David
> *Arrows of Time,* David Vining 1999

Witser, Steve
> *Among Friends,* Albany Records TROY 373

Bass Trombone

Bachmann, Armin
> *Fantastic,* Marcophon CD 892

Bollinger, Blair
> *Fancy Free,* d'Notes Classics DND1033

Knaub, Donald
> *Sound Waves,* Crystal 680
> *Retread,* Donald Knaub 2004

Rojak, John
> *The Romantic Bass Trombone,* MMC Recordings MMC 2098

Vernon, Charles
> *Charles Vernon—Bass Trombone,* Albany Records-Troy 723

Yeo, Doug
> *Tale 1,* Die letzte Posaunne 51955

Jazz

Fontana, Carl
> *Heavyweights,* Mama 1013
> *Nice-N-Easy,* Cambria 1701
> *The Great Fontana,* Uptown 2728

Fuller, Curtis
> *Four on the Outside,* Bellaphon CDSJP 124

Hampton, Slide
> *Roots,* Criss Cross Jazz 1015
> *Mellow-dy,* LRC CDC 9053

Herwig, Conrad
> *The Amulet,* KEN 016
> *The Latin Side of John Coltrane,* Astor Place TCD 4003

Johnson, J. J.
> *The Trombone Master,* Columbia CK 44443
> *The Eminent Jay,* Jay Johnson, vol 1, Blue Note CDP 7 81505 2
> *The Eminent Jay,* Jay Johnson, vol 2, Blue Note CDP 7 81506 2
> *Quintergy,* Antilles 422-848 214-2

McDougall, Ian
> *The Warmth of the Horn,* Concord Jazz CCD-4652

Ory, Kid
> *Kid Ory's Creole Jazz Band 1954,* GoodTime Jazz GTJCD-12004-2

Rosolino, Frank
> *Frank Talks,* Storyville STCD 8284
> *Free for All,* Specialty OJCCD-1763-2

Teagarden, Jack
> *A Hundred Years from Today,* Grudge Music 4523-2-F

Turre, Steve
> *Viewpoints and Vibrations,* Stash Records ST-CD-2
> *In the Spur of the Moment,* Telarc CD-83484

Watrous, Bill
> *Bonefied,* GNP Crescendo GNPD 2211

Whigham, Jiggs
> *The Jiggs Up,* Capri 74024-2

Selected Bibliography

Berret, Joshua and Louis G. Bourgois III. *The Musical World of J.J. Johnson,* Lanham, MD: The Scarecrow Press, 1999.

Dempster, Stuart. *The Modern Trombone: A Definition of its Idioms,* Berkeley: University of California Press, 1979.

Everett, Thomas. *Annotated Guide to Bass Trombone Literature,* Nashville: Brass Press, 1985.

Fasman, Mark I. *Brass Bibliography,* Bloomington and Indianapolis: Indiana University Press, 1990.

Fink, Reginald. *The Trombonists' Handbook,* Athens, OH: Accura Music, 1977.

Gregory, Robin. *The Trombone: The Instrument and Its Music,* London: Faber & Faber, 1973.

Guion, David. *The Trombone: Its History and Music, 1697–1811.* New York: Gordon and Breach, 1988.

Herbert, Trevor and John Wallace, *eds. The Cambridge Companion to Brass Instruments,* Cambridge: Cambridge University Press, 1997.

Kagarice, Vern. *Annotated Guide to Trombone Solos with Band and Orchestra,* Lebanon, IN: studio PR, 1974.

Kagarice, Vern, et al. *Solos for the Student Trombonist,* Nashville: Brass Press, 1979.

Kleinhammer, Edward. *The Art of Trombone Playing,* Evanston, Ill.: Summy-Birchard, 1963.

———. *Mastering the Trombone,* Hannover: Edition Piccolo, 1997.

Knaub, Donald. *Trombone Teaching Techniques,* Fairport, NY: Rochester Music, 1977.

Thompson, J. Mark, ed. *Solos for the Student Trombonist,* 2nd edition, Vuarmarens, Switzerland: Editions BIM, 2004.

Thompson, J. Mark and Jeffrey Lemke. *French Music for Low Brass Instruments,* Bloomington: Indiana University Press, 1994.

Wick, Denis. *Trombone Technique,* London: Oxford University Press, 1973.

Harmonic Series of the Trombone

Trombone Position Chart

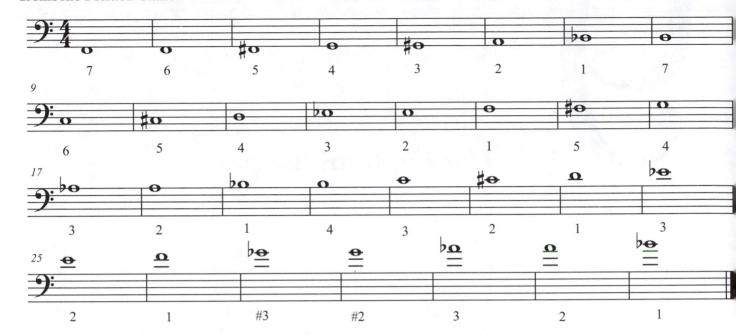

CHAPTER

9

The Euphonium

Because of the similarity of trombone and euphonium embouchures, articulations, breathing specifics, overtone series, and suggested ranges, those topics will not be covered separately in this chapter. The reader may refer to Chapter 8, "The Trombone," for this information.

Terminology is a problem when describing the euphonium. The words *euphonium*, *tenor tuba*, *baritone*, *baritone horn*, and *tenor horn* are often used somewhat interchangeably, despite significant differences among the actual instruments having these names. For the sake of consistency, *euphonium* is used throughout this chapter to describe the instrument properly so called.

The euphonium is the instrument that fills the tenor and baritone range of the valved brasses. Its length is identical to the length of the trombone, and it is also pitched in B-flat. Consequently, its pitch range is the same as that of the tenor trombone. Like the tuba, the euphonium is considered a conical instrument because of its greater proportion of flared to cylindrical tubing. Its relation to the tuba can also be seen in its vertical playing position, its large bore, and its high, tubalike sound. Figure 9–1 shows the euphonium and its parts.

Family of Instruments

Originally, the "baritone horn" was a slightly smaller version of the euphonium, or of the tenor tuba, used in European bands. It is pitched in B-flat but has a smaller bore and a smaller bell, which together produce a somewhat lighter tone quality. It is still in use today, especially in brass bands in Europe and in some service bands in the United States. Throughout this chapter, this instrument will be referred to as the "baritone horn."

The instrument found in most school bands in the United States is also called a "baritone" or "baritone horn." It is a hybrid instrument that has been designed to create a euphoniumlike sound in a smaller instrument. It is well suited to the musical development and cost restrictions of the average school-aged musician.

Figure 9–1 Parts of the Euphonium

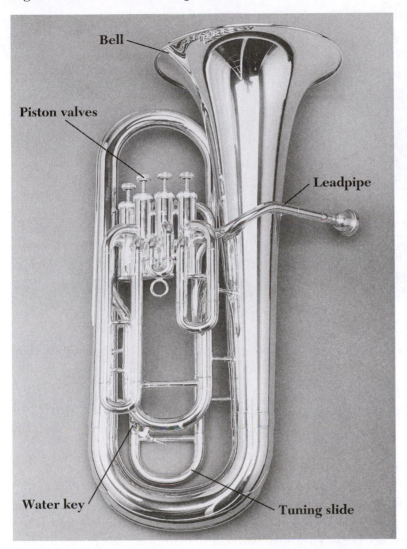

Throughout this chapter, this instrument will be referred to as the "American baritone."

The tenor horn evolved out of the saxhorn tradition of a family of instruments, all with proportionally identical bores that cover the complete tonal range. This instrument has fallen into disuse today.

Baritone or euphonium? Attempts to answer this question have been included in many books, articles, and pamphlets. Even manufacturers disagree about what instrument they are actually producing. Some solutions include the following:

1. Generally, euphoniums are large-bore instruments with large, usually upright, bells.
2. Generally, euphoniums are European- or Japanese-made professional-quality instruments.
3. Generally, euphoniums will have four valves, although some have three. Some baritones have four valves.

Figure 9–2   Family of Instruments

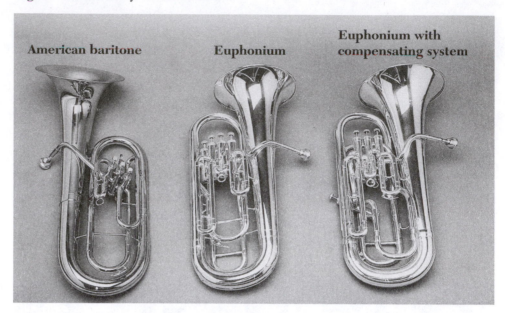

4. Euphoniums do not have a reversible main tuning slide—the tubing will flare so that one side is larger than the other. Baritones generally have a reversible main tuning slide.

The various instruments related to the euphonium are shown in Figure 9–2.

Student Qualifications

From school to school, differing philosophies regarding beginning students on the euphonium are found. Some teachers believe that the instrument is too large for the average beginner to play, carry, and maintain. Others believe that the instrument is well suited to the beginner because of its moderate-sized mouthpiece and ease of tone production. Whatever the decision of the teacher, the prospective euphonium player should be screened for normal dental, lung, and lip formations.

As with the trombone, horn, and tuba, "overstocked" sections of the band can provide willing candidates to switch to euphonium. Often, trumpet players will make good euphonium players. Many band pieces are provided with treble clef euphonium parts (in B-flat) so that the new player need not learn new fingerings and can begin playing instantly. When this is the case, the following should be observed:

1. Because of the larger mouthpiece, there is a very common tendency for the new euphonium student to allow the bottom lip to protrude too far into the mouthpiece, causing the air to be blown upward. This is very limiting and should be monitored carefully.
2. The volume of air used when playing the euphonium is much larger than the amount needed to play the trumpet. The new player should be encouraged to breathe deeply and blow freely to create the characteristic euphonium sound.

3. Because most advanced euphonium solo, étude, and band literature is available only in bass clef, all euphonium players should begin reading bass clef as soon as possible.

Proper Hand and Holding Positions

Right-hand Position

The fingers of the right hand operate the three (sometimes four) valves of the euphonium. It is not necessary to keep the fingers curved so that the tips of the fingers are pressing the valves. Because the valves are bigger and farther apart than trumpet valves, curving the fingers actually creates tension and limits flexibility. The fingers should be curved slightly as if the player were holding a softball, so that the pads of the fingers are used to depress the valves.

If the little finger is not used for the fourth valve, it should be allowed to move freely with the third finger. The thumb should also be allowed as much freedom as possible. Thumb rings and braces should be used only as points of contact for the thumb. Relaxation and flexibility must be maintained in the right hand.

Figure 9–3 shows the correct position of the right hand on the euphonium.

Left-hand Position

There is no single function of the left hand. Its use is dictated by the particular physical characteristics of the instrument. On most euphoniums, the left hand steadies the instrument while the player is seated, and it holds most of the weight when the player is standing. On some euphoniums, the fourth valve is located on the lower-left side (viewed from the front) and must be operated by a finger on the left hand. Main and valve tuning slides can be adjusted by the left hand while

Figure 9–3   Right-hand Position

Figure 9–4   Left-hand Position

playing. Regardless of where the left hand is placed, it is important that the instrument is held comfortably and the body is relaxed.

Figure 9–4 illustrates the position of the left hand on the euphonium.

Posture

The manner in which the euphonium is held will vary almost as much as does the left-hand placement. Regardless of whether the player is seated or standing, the mouthpiece must be brought up to the player's lips. Any ducking of the head or craning of the neck affects the inhalation and exhalation process and will create unnecessary tension.

When the instrument is rested on the lap of younger students, the mouthpiece is invariably situated well above the embouchure. A simple solution is to angle the instrument slightly so that the mouthpiece and embouchure meet comfortably. When an older student is in a seated position, the mouthpiece often reaches just up to the chin or lower. Use a small pillow in the player's lap or a guitar footstand for the left leg to raise the euphonium to the proper height. A special euphonium stand is also available for this purpose.

Figure 9–5 shows the sitting position for playing the euphonium.

When standing, as in a solo performance situation, it is important to bring the mouthpiece to the lips. The weight of the instrument must be held in the left hand. Supporting with the right hand produces tension and rigidity. It is also important to keep the breathing apparatus open and flexible by not pressing the instrument into the body. Standing positions should be encouraged only in older, physically mature students because of the extreme weight of the instrument.

Intonation Tendencies

Like all valved brasses, the euphonium has inherent intonation problems when valves are used in combination. Unlike the other brasses, the euphonium usually

Figure 9–5   Sitting Position

has no mechanical means by which to offset these problems. The fourth valve and compensating system offer some relief, but only in the lower range. The euphonium player must take the time to learn the pitch tendencies of the instrument very well. Careful practice with an electronic tuner will demonstrate visually what the player will be required to hear. Armed with this information, the euphonium player will find it necessary to bend or lip the pitches much more than performers on the other brasses. This tends to cause fatigue in the embouchure but must become a natural habit for the player.

Like the trombonist, the euphonium player must have a daily routine with which to refine fundamental techniques. In addition to the exercises suggested in Chapter 8, euphonium players should add daily practice in facility. Some special warm-up exercises are shown in Figure 9–6.

Choosing a Euphonium and Euphonium Equipment

Instruments

Baritones and euphoniums are manufactured with two bell orientations—bell up and bell front. The bell-front models tend to send the sound in a more linear

Figure 9–6   Warm-up Exercises
Long Tones

Lip Slurs   Play on all valve combinations.

Tonguing   Play in all major and minor keys.

Begin on all pitches in a chromatic octave.

direction, like a trumpet or trombone, and are used quite often in marching situations. The bell-up models tend to diffuse the sound, much like a tuba, and are recommended for most solo and ensemble situations.

American Baritones

Most manufacturers make a beginning-model American baritone. These instruments are somewhat expensive when compared with similar-quality trumpets and trombones. Many schools provide these instruments for beginning students. Recommended American baritones include the following:

>Bach 1566
>Yamaha YEP-211
>Conn 141, 151
>King 625, 627

Euphoniums

True euphoniums are available in several price and quality ranges. Most are available in lacquer or silver plate; all are available with four valves. The fourth valve is a requisite for any quality euphonium. Unlike the trumpet and horn, there are no devices or techniques available to facilitate the correction of the inherent pitch problems of valves. The fourth valve can be tuned so that it replaces the sharp 1–3 combination with a true pitch. Other combinations with the fourth valve are shown later in this chapter.

The following recommended instruments are listed in order of least to most expensive; an asterisk indicates the inclusion of a compensating system.

>Yamaha YEP-321   Besson 967*, 968*
>Willson 2704   Willson 2901*
>Yamaha YEP-621   Hirsbrunner*
>Yamaha YEP-641*

Mouthpieces

Even though trombone mouthpieces can be used to play the euphonium, mouthpieces that are slightly deeper than trombone mouthpieces work better on euphonium. These mouthpieces provide a darker, deeper tone quality characteristic of the euphonium.

Like the trombone mouthpieces, these mouthpieces come with large and small shanks. Generally, the large shanks are for the professional-level instruments, and the small shanks are for baritones and some euphoniums. Some British manufacturers used to produce a leadpipe that worked only with an in-between-size shank. Adapters are available for these. Adapters are also available for joining a small shank to a large receiver, but these should be avoided.

Recommended Mouthpieces, Beginner

>Bach 11, 7
>Schilke (Yamaha) 46D-48

Recommended Mouthpieces, Intermediate

>Bach 6½ AL
>Schilke 50
>Denis Wick 6AL

Recommended Mouthpieces, Advanced

>Schilke 51, 51D
>Denis Wick 5AL, 4½AL, 4AL

The Compensating System

The compensating system is an attempt to alleviate the intonation problems of valves used in combination. Simply put, when the fourth valve is engaged with another valve, the air column is sent back through a different, shorter set of valve tubing (located on the back of the valve assembly) that adds the acoustically necessary lengths to lower the sharp combinations. This system also allows the complete chromatic range below E to B-flat below the staff.

To determine whether a euphonium has a compensating system, seek out an area professional or a local music store. By showing them the instrument or giving them the manufacturer and a model number, they will be able to tell you whether it has a compensating system. Typically, euphoniums without a compensating system will have three valves, or in the case of a four-valve instrument, all four valves will be in a row near the top. Only four-valve euphoniums may have a compensating system; those instruments will have the fourth valve located away from the other three valves, low on the side of the instrument near the third valve slide.

Mutes

Occasionally, usually only in advanced literature, the euphonium is required to play with a mute. Straight mutes are used most often.

Recommended Euphonium Mutes

> Denis Wick
> Humes and Berg fiber (bell up and bell front)

Cleaning and Maintaining the Euphonium

For care and maintenance procedures, refer to Chapter 10, "The Tuba." When cleaning euphonium valves, refer to Chapter 6, "The Trumpet."

History of the Euphonium

The origins of the baritone and euphonium can be found in the early nineteenth century. This was an important time for brass instruments because of the great amount of experimentation in instrument design and production taking place. Valves were invented and different-shaped instruments appeared. Efforts at producing a tenor- or baritone-voiced instrument during that time included instruments such as the flicorno basso, quinticlave, herculesophone, saxtromba, baroxyton, phonicon, bassflugelhorn, althorn, bombardon, and baryton.

Adolphe Sax invented the family of saxhorns in the mid-nineteenth century. These were a complete family of valved brasses voiced from soprano to bass, including tenor and baritone instruments. In addition, as the tuba was evolving through the nineteenth century, manufacturers would often produce a tenor version of the tuba, called "tenortuba" (1838) by Moritz; "euphonion" (1843) by Sommer, whose instrument was also known as the sommerphone; and "baroxyton" (1848) by Cerveny.

The baritone and euphonium as we know them today were logical outgrowths of these early efforts. The fact that there is currently no typical size or shape, combined with the continuous improvements being made to these instruments, indicates that the baritone and euphonium are still in a state of evolution today.

Graded Literature Lists

Method Books, Beginning

Arban/Randall	Complete Method
Clarke/Gordon	Technical Studies
Fink	From Treble to Bass Clef

Method Books, Intermediate

Bleger	31 Brilliant Studies
Blume	36 Studies
Bordogni/Rochut	Melodious Études, Books I and 2
Fink	Introducing Tenor Clef
Kopprasch	60 Studies, Book I
Voxman	Selected Studies

Method Books, Advanced

Bitsch	15 Études de Rythme
Blazevich	Clef Studies
Couillard	40 Modern Studies
Ostrander	Shifting Meter Studies
Slama	66 Études
Tyrrell	40 Progressive Studies

Grades 1–4 Solo Literature

Refer to the corresponding list of literature for the trombone in Chapter 8.

Grade 5 Solo Literature

Barat	Andante et Allegro
Bush	Recitative, Arioso, and Polonaise
Clarke, H. L.	Bride of the Waves
Clarke, H. L.	Carnival of Venice
Guilmant	Morceau Symphonique
Hovhaness	Concerto no. 3
Hutchison	Sonatina
Kryzwicki	Ballade
Tomasi	Danse Sacrée

Grade 6 Solo Literature

Adler	Four Dialogues (Bass Trombone)
Bach, Jan	Concert Variants
Curnow	Symphonic Variants
George	Sonata
Hovhaness	Symphony no. 29
Jacob	Fantasia
Ross	Capriccio Furioso
Ross	Partita
Townsend	Chamber Concerto no.2
White	Lyric Suite
Wilder	Concerto
Wilder	Sonata

Many solos originally for cornet are often performed on euphonium. Refer to the works of Herbert Clarke, and others, in Chapter 6.

Selected Discography

Baglin, Lyndon
    Showcase for the Euphonium, Saydisc 269
Bowman, Brian
    Brian Bowman, Crystal S393

Dart, Fred
    Euphonium Solos, Coronet 850C- 7275
Droste, Paul
    Artist in Residence, Coronet LPS 3026

Falcone, Leonard
  Falcone and His Baritone, Golden Crest RE7001
Matteson, Rich
  Sounds of the WASP, ASI 203
Nelson, Douglas
  Recital Music, Mark MRS 37878

Young, Raymond
  Clinician Series, Golden Crest CR 1009
  Raymond Young, Century 17647
  Raymond Young, Baritone Horn, Golden Crest RE 7025

Selected Bibliography

Bevan, Clifford. *The Tuba Family,* London: Faber & Faber, 1978.

Bowman, Brian L. *Practical Hints on Playing the Baritone (Euphonium),* Melville, N.Y.: Belwin Mills, 1983.

Griffiths, John R. *The Low Brass Guide,* Hackensack, N.J.: Jerona Music Corp., 1980.

Louder, Earl L., and David R. Corbin. *Euphonium Music Guide,* Evanston, Ill.: The Instrumentalist, 1978.

Morris, R. Winston. *Tuba Music Guide,* Evanston, Ill.: The Instrumentalist, 1973.

Rose, William. *Studio Class Manual for Tuba and Euphonium,* Houston, Tex.: Iola Publications, 1980.

Winter, Denis. *Euphonium Music Guide,* New Haven, Conn.: Whaling Music Publishers, n.d.

Harmonic Series of the Euphonium

| 0 | 2 | 1 | 1–2 (3) | 2–3 | 1–3 (4) | 1–2–3 (2–4) |

Fingering Chart, Euphonium
°indicates compensating system

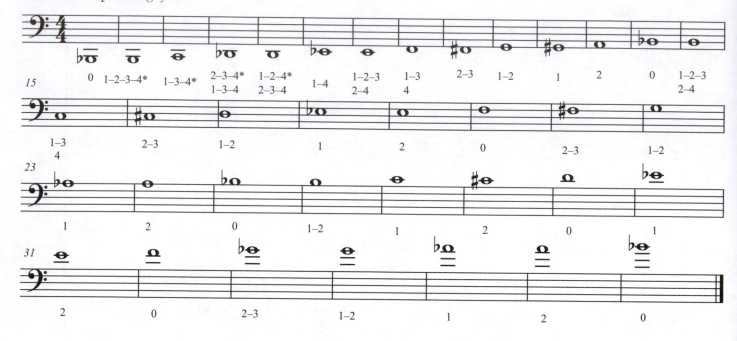

The Tuba

The tuba is the bass voice of the brass family. Like the horn and euphonium, it is a conical-bore instrument; it is the conical bore that gives the tuba its characteristically large, resonant sound. The shortest configuration of the BB-flat tuba is approximately 18 feet, twice the length of the trombone and euphonium, placing the fundamental exactly one octave below. The tuba uses a cup-shaped mouthpiece.

The size of the tuba varies more than that of the other brasses. Bell diameters vary from 14 inches to more than 20 inches. Bore diameters vary from approximately 0.630 to 0.850 inch. These differences allow for varying ease of playing as well as varying tone colors.

A concern among many music educators is the potential loss of the tuba from music programs. In this chapter, considerable attention is given to transferring students from another instrument to tuba. By following the suggestions in this chapter, the educator will be able to successfully transfer a student to tuba—or start a new student on tuba—at any age. Students can start on tuba or transfer to tuba as late as high school, although it is preferable to do so in early junior high or middle school.

Transferring may even be preferred to starting the instrument at the grade school level. Some educators advocate transferring students to tuba over starting the instrument at the grade school level even though there can be significant problems inherent in transferring students to the tuba. However, if problems are solved at an early point, the student can and should be expected to perform and improve as well as a student of any other instrument.

Instruments of the Tuba Family

The BB-flat Tuba

The BB-flat tuba is the most common instrument in the tuba family. This instrument is used mostly by public school systems and by nonprofessionals who continue playing beyond their school career. It is the choice for public

Figure 10–1   Parts of the Tuba

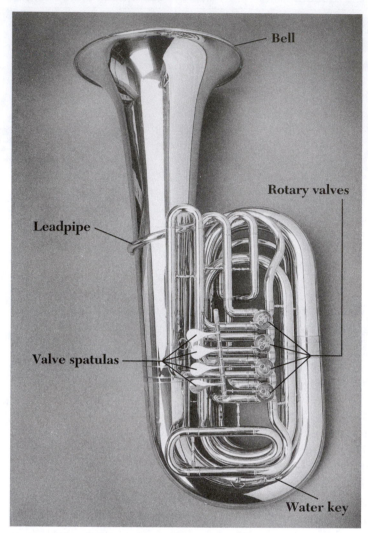

schools because of its key—most other brass instruments in the school systems are keyed in B-flat—and because most manufacturers build BB-flat tubas with durability in mind to withstand the grueling, rough treatment of young tubists. The BB-flat tuba and its parts are illustrated in Figure 10–1.

The CC Tuba

The CC tuba is the choice of professional tubists and serious advanced students. It is keyed in C, one whole step above the BB-flat tuba. The CC tuba is generally a more refined instrument, built for responsiveness and not for durability. The fingering patterns on the CC tuba are more comfortable in the sharp keys, and for that reason C has been the preferred instrument among professionals.

The E-flat Tuba

The E-flat tuba is a smaller tuba keyed a perfect fourth above the BB-flat tuba. This instrument gained its popularity in England in brass bands. It is not used extensively, except for the few public schools that use it for their younger students and the professionals who use it in orchestras, in chamber ensembles, or for solo work. However, its popularity has been increasing over the last two decades.

The F Tuba

The F tuba is pitched a whole step above the E-flat tuba; it is used extensively by professionals and serious advanced students. The smaller size of the instrument gives a lighter, brighter sound that enhances the higher orchestral parts, and its clarity of sound is preferred for solo and chamber works.

The Sousaphone

The sousaphone is a form of tuba built for ease of carrying in marching situations. It is most often keyed in B-flat, but some are pitched in E-flat. The original sousaphone was keyed in C. Some sousaphones are made partly of fiberglass, and although these instruments are lighter to carry, their quality of sound is less desirable than that of the brass instruments. The sousaphone is illustrated in Figure 10–2.

The Euphonium

The euphonium is sometimes referred to as a "tenor tuba." Although its design is similar to that of the tuba, it is still a unique instrument, with a slightly different approach to playing. Most advanced and professional tuba players double on the euphonium and at times perform with the instrument in orchestras and chamber ensembles.

Figure 10–2   The Sousaphone

Student Qualifications; Transferring Students to Tuba

Whether to find a student to begin tuba as his or her first instrument or to transfer a student of another instrument is a decision that should be made carefully. This section addresses the needs of the student and the ensemble for both the beginner and the transfer.

It is not necessary for the beginning student to be large, but the student must be able to hold the instrument with the correct posture. Therefore, it is very important to have the proper-sized equipment available. Recommendations will be discussed later in this chapter. Some teachers believe that fuller lips are better suited for the tuba. There do not seem to be sufficient grounds to substantiate this theory.

No special aptitude is required for a student to play the tuba, but it is an advantage to be able to differentiate low pitches easily. Unless the student has a physical ear deficiency, most students will learn to hear the low sounds effectively. As with any other instrument, the desire to succeed is the most important attribute.

There is some controversy over when to start a student on the tuba. Some educators believe that the young student will not be physically developed enough to handle the instrument, and others believe that transferring has too many inherent problems. Both of these problems can be solved by having the proper equipment on hand and by correct teaching techniques.

To identify a candidate for transfer to the tuba

1. Know which instruments are easiest to transfer from.
2. Identify students who are likely to succeed.
3. Interview the prospective student personally.
4. Work individually with the student.

The saxophone is an excellent instrument from which to transfer. Generally, students who have a "woofy" sound on saxophone will make the change more easily. The basic characteristics of the saxophone embouchure—firm corners, a fairly soft "pad," and an open throat—bear enough similarities to the tuba embouchure that the student will be able to adjust fairly quickly. Also, a saxophone student will have had exposure to complex rhythms, phrasing, and technical passages. Some saxophonists will have experience dealing with an instrument change if they have at some point played tenor or baritone saxophone in addition to alto. These students may be more willing and have an easier time making the transfer. Transferring from the euphonium or trombone can be very successful. The embouchures are the closest to the tuba of any brass instrument, as are the similarities in the airstream.

Changing from percussion can be successful because there is no previous embouchure to change. The only advantage for the percussionist over a new student is the familiarity with notes and rhythms and the experience in ensemble playing.

Transferring from the horn can work well. Even though the embouchure is much more closed on the horn, the instrument covers a large range, and the concepts for the lower range on the horn are similar to tuba. Obviously, it is best to choose a student who has a strong low register; often this will coincide with a weak upper register. Further, there are similarities in the basic sound characteristics between the horn and tuba that will aid the student in the transfer process.

Transferring from trumpet is very problematic and not recommended, yet it is a popular choice. The trumpet embouchure is considerably tighter and much more rigid; the oral cavity is smaller, the tongue placement is much higher, and the air stream is much more focused and compressed than on a tuba. Although at first glance the embouchures and general approach may seem similar, these differences, which are in reality quite large, are very difficult for the young player to conceptualize and realize, even with regular private instruction. However, the student with the proper attitude can overcome these issues. Choose a transfer from trumpet with great care.

The double-reed instruments and clarinet also have potentially serious problems that can cause more work than necessary for the educator. Chief among them are a stiff "pad," lips that are rolled back over the teeth, and a highly compressed airflow. Certainly, it is possible to successfully transfer from these instruments, but, like the trumpet, it is less than optimal and may require more attention from the instructor to make the transfer successful.

Attitude is the most important factor to consider when choosing a transfer student. The ideal student is one who is working at an instrument but not fulfilling his or her expectations. This will probably be a student in the middle of the section. This type of student will be easier to persuade to transfer, and if this student has the desire to succeed, you can almost guarantee success.

After you have identified students suitable for transfer, interview them individually and explain the reasons why you believe they will succeed on and enjoy playing the tuba. Often students are asked to transfer to tuba with no explanation and no real encouragement. Give the student recordings of professional tuba players.

Even with proper encouragement, transferring to a new instrument can seem a daunting task and one many students will resist. Understandably, most students don't want to leave the comfort of their old instrument. For these students, persuade them to put the other instrument aside for just a few weeks to give the tuba a fair try. With reassurances that they may return to their old instrument, the natural resistance students show may be easily sidestepped. After a student gets a small measure of comfort on the tuba, they are usually happy to stay.

Take time to teach the student personally for the first few weeks. Your investment at this stage will give the student more confidence in your decision. The first two to three weeks is crucial. At this time, the student will start to get comfortable with and form the basis for the new techniques. Although all the bad habits will not be fixed during this time, a philosophy of how to approach the tuba and its idiosyncrasies—and a solid, practical foundation for producing a reasonable sound—can be achieved. After this initial period, the student should go to a tuba teacher whose primary instrument is tuba, preferably one who has had experience with transfers.

It is almost guaranteed that students left to practice alone during the early part of the transfer will develop severe problems. Therefore, the students should practice with supervision until they are comfortable with the new concepts. Further, it is not recommended to put a student into the ensemble until he or she has a measure of solidity. The pressure to "keep up" will encourage quick fixes to developmental issues, forcing the creation of bad habits. If possible, have an older student or teacher aid work with the student during rehearsals.

It is usually best to teach the new technical ideas by using analogies. If you focus your time on controlling the many small, individual aspects of the embouchure, air, and oral cavity, the student may become overwhelmed and never be able to absorb all these intricate ideas. Start with the large concepts—free flowing, energetic air, large volumes of air without excessive effort, open oral set as in saying "ah" or "oe"—and then work toward the smaller concepts.

Assembly

Most tubas do not require assembly except for placing the mouthpiece in the receiver. Never allow the student to pound the mouthpiece into the receiver. A gentle twist will secure the mouthpiece in place.

The sousaphone and a few tubas have removable bell sections. Students should learn the following procedure:

1. Place the bell section into the receiver.
2. Position the bell to the desired position (on sousaphones).
3. Gently tighten the screws around the receiver. The screw mechanism will be severely damaged if tightened to the extreme. A fingertip firmness should be sufficient.

Proper Hand and Holding Positions

Posture

Proper posture is important for all aspects of playing, especially breathing. The player should sit comfortably straight in the chair, not stiff or extended. The mouthpiece should meet the embouchure without the need for the student to reach or slouch. It may be necessary to seat the student on a book if the tuba is too tall, or for the student to rest the tuba on the lap if he or she is too tall. Devices designed to support the tuba (the Stewart Stand, for example) can work well if they do not rigidly hold the tuba. Students must be able to move and situate the instrument to fit their posture; static devices force the student to adjust their posture to the stand.

Figure 10–3 shows the sitting position used with rotary-valve tubas, and Figure 10–4 shows the sitting position for piston-valve tubas. Figure 10–5 illustrates the standing position for playing the sousaphone.

Hand Positions

There are two basic constructions of the "concert" instrument. The most common in school use has the valves on the left side of the leadpipe as you face the instrument. With this type, the right arm is behind the instrument with the fingertips on the valves, fingers slightly arched. The thumb opposes the index finger and rests below the tubing behind the valves. See Figure 10–7. The right forearm should be raised at about a 45-degree angle to the floor. The left hand is in front of the instrument, gently supporting the tuba and in a position that allows access to as many tuning slides as possible.

For tubas with the valve section to the right of the leadpipe as you face the instrument, the right hand is in front of the instrument with the fingertips on the platters or valves, fingers slightly arched, with the thumb placed in or near the thumb ring. The left hand is over the top bow of the tuba, gently grasping

Figure 10–3   Sitting Position Rotary Valve   **Figure 10–4**

Figure 10–5

**Figure 10–6   Hand
Positions for Rotary Valve**

the first and, generally, the third valve slide. The left forearm should be approx-imately parallel with the floor.

For the sousaphone, the left hand reaches around the tubing near the left shoulder and gently supports the neck. The right arm lies against the tubing near the hip, and the fingers of the right hand are slightly arched over the valves. Figure 10–6 shows the hand positions for rotary-valve tubas, and Figure 10–7 gives the hand positions for piston-valve tubas.

Embouchure Specifics

Most tubists agree that the embouchure should be centered in the mouthpiece both vertically and horizontally. Some variation is accepted, as long as it is kept to a minimum.

Proper Tuba Embouchure

The following steps will help the student form the correct embouchure:

1. Keep the lips gently touching as if humming, and slightly forward.

Figure 10–7 Hand Positions for Piston Valve

2. The jaw is low, relaxed, and very slightly forward. Placing a finger between the teeth will result in the proper position.
3. The tongue is very low and flat on the bottom of the oral cavity, as in saying "ah" or "oe." The tip and sides should be below the bottom teeth. This is true for most of the range of the instrument. In the extreme upper register (approaching an octave above middle c) many performers will arch their tongue into an "ay" position.
4. The throat remains very open and relaxed in all registers.
5. The chin is flat and relaxed, not bunched or rigidly flexed.
6. The muscles around the lips are slightly forward to create a cushion for the mouthpiece to rest on. Keep an equal, gentle pressure on both lips.
7. The corners are firm and slightly forward, never "puffed out" away from the teeth. The correct embouchure for the tuba is shown in Figure 10–8.

As with all wind instruments, proper formation of the embouchure is most important. Most problems on the tuba are the result of an incorrectly formed embouchure. Those students who have learned the correct embouchure will exhibit technique on the level of the better trumpet students.

Unlike the trumpet and most other wind instruments that use the tongue extensively to manipulate the airsteam, the tuba will usually focus and manipulate the airstream at the embouchure. Consequently, the only point of resistance for the airstream on the tuba is at the lips.

Figure 10–8   Embouchure of the Tuba

Many tuba professors, the author included, believe that tuba embouchure is driven primarily by the lower lip. In the lower registers the lower lip is more prominent and may actually "pout" slightly out from the upper lip, and in the upper registers it is flatter and more even with, perhaps even behind, the upper. An analogy is blowing upward slightly in the lower registers and downward in the upper. Please take careful note: at no time should either of the lips be rolled back over or behind the teeth.

Some players will naturally manipulate their lower lip in the mouthpiece with little outward sign; others will pivot around the mouthpiece in various ways. Pivoting helps keep equal pressure on the embouchure as the lower jaw moves back and forth to allow the lower lip to do its job. To allow the lower jaw to move forward so the lower lip is accentuated for the lower registers, the head needs to slightly tilt downward—the lower lip should not slide down the mouthpiece. Gently rocking back with the instrument can help, or pivoting the head slightly. For the upper registers, leaning slightly forward or pivoting the head up slightly will allow the jaw to move backward. The movement should be small and smooth. It is not recommended that this technique be summarily taught; however, allow it to continue if it is noticed, or use it as an aid if a student is having difficulties with the low register and other avenues have been exhausted.

Techniques specifically used to develop the embouchure without the instrument should be used with caution, especially at the beginning stages.

1. Extensive lip buzzing is not recommended for the beginner. Young students and transfers may develop tension in the embouchure and airstream. Because there is little resistance when buzzing in the mouthpiece alone, students are uncomfortable with the huge volumes of air needed to make the lips buzz and will often resort to a small, tight aperture to restrict the air loss.

However, in short doses with the students understanding that they should lose their air very quickly (up to eight times faster than on a trumpet mouthpiece), it can be an excellent learning tool.

2. Visualizer buzzing may be substituted for lip buzzing. The visualizer will help the young student to focus the embouchure and airstream without added tension. Carefully monitor the embouchure, oral cavity, and airstream while using the visualizer.

3. Although mouthpiece buzzing can be detrimental especially to the young player, with proper supervision and for the more advanced students it is one of the best embouchure exercises. A "fuzzy," slightly airy sound on the mouthpiece will create a large, energetic, rich sound on the instrument. The buzz on the tuba mouthpiece is not like that of the other brass. For instance, the trumpet buzz will be much more intense and focused than the tuba buzz.

Embouchure Problems

The largest and most common problem for tuba students, especially transfer students, is tension in the embouchure. Students may develop a "smile" embouchure or pinch the airsteam in an attempt to either restrict air loss or create enough air speed for the upper registers. As the embouchure becomes more restricted, students find that they need to force the airstream, which creates a harsh, nasal sound, and as the vibrating surface of the lips gets thinner and less dense, the sound will lose resonance and fullness.

Transfers from woodwind instruments often roll the lower lip back over the bottom lip. This causes problems in getting to the lower range and gives the upper range a harsh, unfocused sound. Have the student gently roll out the lips.

Other characteristics that may be associated with an improper embouchure are "puffed-out" cheeks (Figure 10–9) and a "tucked" lower lip (Figure 10–10).

Figure 10–9   Puffed Cheeks

**Figure 10–10   Tucked
Lower Lip**

Articulation

Tonguing

Basic tonguing on the tuba is unusual compared with the other brasses. The tongue must remain low in the mouth, and the throat must be open at all times. The distance the tongue has to travel is very large. The movement in the lower register is back and forth; however, tonguing in the upper register is similar to tonguing on the trombone, with a more up-and-down movement. The syllables used in the basic articulation for the lower register are "thoe," "thu," or "tha," and for the upper register, "toe," "tu," or "ta." The student must find the most natural way to articulate. The syllables will vary slightly for each student. The "oe" and "u" vowels are preferred because they tend to keep the lips forward. The use of the "th" consonant is to demonstrate tongue placement. No air should pass the tongue when it is placed in this setting. Refer to exercises 9C, 9D, 10A, 10B, 11B, 13A, 13C, 15B, 16B, 21D, and 22C for practice using single tonguing.

Legato Style

The placement of the tongue during the legato articulation is farther back than for the basic articulation. Use the syllables "noe," "nu," "na" or "doe," "du," "da." The tongue uses much more of an up-and-down movement in this articulation.

Slur and Lip Slur

The slur is always a smooth action for the embouchure and airstream. The following steps should be used to ensure a proper approach to slurring:

1. The lips gently and smoothly focus the airstream. There should be no obstruction of the air at any point. To slur up, the air is focused smaller ("cooler" air), and to slur down, the air stream is opened.

2. The airstream must be "energized" when slurring up to compensate for the added resistance of the smaller aperture and to increase the airspeed so the lip vibrates faster. As the focus opens for the lower notes, the airstream relaxes somewhat—it must still have energy—while the volume of air increases. The proper approach to the airstream is discussed later in the chapter.

The slur is a difficult concept for the young tubist to master. Generally, time and encouragement of good slur habits is all that is needed. In short, it is the requirement to make a clean, artful slur very quickly that will push students into finding quick fixes to the problems. In almost all cases these quick fixes are limiting and will actually inhibit the development of a good slur. Fortunately, most of the quick fixes are predictable and correctable. Still, it is best to take time at the beginning so the student has the comfort he or she needs to adequately develop a feel for slurring. The following list describes some of the more common "tricks" used to hide problems with slurs:

1. "Puffing" the air. An excessive expulsion of air occurs at the beginning of each new note, especially when slurring up. The student is avoiding the "garbled" part of the slur as he or she moves from one note to the next by "punching" the air to quickly force out the new note. Although this is the least insidious of the "tricks," it is a habit that will restrict smoothness and facility. To help alleviate this, allow the student to make some bad slurs while encouraging the aspect you want him or her to keep.
2. Articulating with the throat. This articulation has a softer attack than the basic "toe" articulation and consequently is much easier to hide from the instructor. Similar to the puffing, it allows the student to hide the "garbled" aspect in the articulation and in some cases the student will puff the air as well. As with the puffing, allow the student to make some bad slurs while encouraging the proper approach.
3. Articulating with the lip. This articulation is similar in response, effect, and corrective strategies to the throat articulation. Students will use a "poe" syllable. This is the least common of the tricks.

Refer to exercises 7A, 7B, 7C, 7D, 22D, 27A, 27B, 29A, 29D, 38A, 39A, 40A, 47D, and 53A for lip slur studies.

Multiple Tonguing

Students should be ready to learn multiple tonguing by the intermediate stage. Both double and triple tonguing are used. The syllables used for multiple tonguing are "thoe" and "koe." It is best to teach the "koe" syllable by itself before it is grouped with the "thoe." Do not start in the low register; instead, use an E-flat or F scale. Tonguing in the low register with a "koe" syllable is difficult and will frustrate the student and lead to the formation of bad habits. Major problems of multiple tonguing are similar to those in basic tonguing, with a few additions:

1. At the beginning stage, be concerned with the relaxation and openness of the throat and tongue and the steady movement of air through the group of notes. As with basic tonguing, this will nearly eliminate the bad habits.
2. The largest problem will be the treatment of the "koe" syllable. Most often the vowel will be distorted and strained. After the student is comfortable with the "koe" syllable, you can then draw attention to other specifics, such

as the crispness of the articulation, grouping the two syllables together: "thoe-koe," "thoe-thoe-koe," and so forth.

3. Tension is another common problem. Students will stiffen the tongue and "hammer" it into place inside the oral cavity. This will often lead to a "tee-kee" placement of the vowels. Although this may be close to where a trumpet player places the tongue, it will cause the sound on a tuba to thin out dramatically and, in severe cases, almost disappear.

A strategy that may help students with the more difficult aspect of the multiple tongue is having them group each type of articulation separately. Using an E-flat or F scale, articulate four times with a basic articulation, followed by four notes with the "koe" articulation; then move to the next note in the scale and repeat. Proceed up and down the scale. When the student has the two types sounding reasonably similar, group them together. Refer to exercises 40D, 46D, 48B, 49C, 49D, 50C, 51C, 53D for practice using double tonguing. Refer to exercises 38D, 50D, 51B, 52C, and 53C for practice using triple tonguing.

Flutter Tonguing

Flutter tonguing is an effect often used in jazz or contemporary music. The jaw should be relaxed and low, the throat open. The tongue may be slightly higher in the mouth than usual for this technique. To produce the sound, the student must use a rolled *r* syllable while exhaling. A common problem with flutter tonguing is that the embouchure and airstream become tense and forced. A reminder that relaxation is the primary concern will help alleviate the problem.

Breath Control

Breath control on the tuba is rarely discussed until a student is a more advanced player or until a problem develops. Basic concepts of good breath control were discussed in Chapter 3, "The Embouchure." This section is added to point out the differences in breath control between the tuba and the other brasses. The volume of air used to support the tuba's sound is very large, and the inhalation and exhalation must be relaxed.

Inhalation

Inhalation is often the least understood aspect of the breathing process for the tuba. If the student is inhaling properly, the shape of the oral cavity will be the same as is used with the proper embouchure. There must be no obstruction of the air during the inhalation. Many teachers recommend that the student inhale from the corners of the mouth. This is not optimal for the tuba. The jaw must drop to allow enough air to flow freely, but not far enough to extend below the mouthpiece.

Exhalation

The exhalation process is very similar for the tuba and the trombone:

1. The airstream for the tuba has no resistance points except for the embouchure.

2. The air column has a wide focus and, although relaxed, is still energetic. Many students, especially transfers, try to squeeze out the air as if blowing through a straw. Indeed, the airstream is considerably more open and may more closely fit the analogy of blowing on a burn or blowing across a soft drink bottle.
3. The volume used is very large and never forced.
4. The air originates from the lower part of the lungs.

The most common air-related issue, especially among transfers, is getting comfortable with the huge volume of air required to support a vibrant sound on the tuba. This is further exacerbated by the fact that as the tuba descends in range, the volume of air increases exponentially: for every octave the tuba lowers, the volume doubles. Getting the student comfortable with this idea does not take a lot of time, but it does take persistence. Encourage young tubists to breathe often. This may happen as much as eight times more often than for the trumpet player, depending on range, dynamics, and the size and efficiency of the student.

Beginning the First Tone

The corresponding section in Chapter 8, "The Trombone," is also an excellent approach for the tuba, with the following considerations:

1. Instead of buzzing the lips alone, have the student "flap" the lips alone, making a sound like a horse. Carefully monitor the tongue placement, because most students will place the tip of the tongue on the roof of the mouth. This technique, although not creating a typical-looking embouchure, will help the student to get an idea of the amount of air needed to produce a high-quality sound.
2. The student should not buzz the mouthpiece at the beginning stage. As discussed earlier, this can lead to tension and a reduction of air movement. Move directly to resonating in the instrument. As the student becomes more comfortable with the amount of air needed, judicious use of mouthpiece buzzing can be included.

The transfer student may have preconceived ideas about the airstream, embouchure, and articulation that need to be adjusted to play the tuba. The lower range will be the most difficult for transfers. Most often they cannot play below the staff, but their high range can carry them well above the staff. If the low range does not work, suggest to the student that the lips be rolled in slightly. This should bring the lips and corners slightly forward while relaxing the vibrating surface.

Many transfer students force the airstream. This will increase tension in the embouchure and further restrict their low range.

The Overtone Series of the BB-flat Tuba

The intonation tendencies resulting from the nature of the overtone series and the characteristics of all valve combinations are identical to those of the trumpets. The

Figure 10–11   Overtone Series of the BB-flat Tuba

principles used to play in tune on the tuba are the same as on the trombone. The valve-tuning slides on the tuba are used like the trombone uses its slide for tuning.

Figure 10–11 illustrates the overtone series for the BB-flat tuba.

Intonation Tendencies

Extra Valves

Many tubas are equipped with a fourth valve. This valve serves the same function as the trigger on the trombone. It was designed primarily to allow the BB-flat tuba to play chromatically below an E. It can be used as an alternative fingering for the 1–3 valve combination, and because it is built flat, it will be closer to the desired intonation. Because of the acoustics of the instrument, the notes below the E will become progressively sharper as the player approaches the fundamental. The notes below an E-flat should be fingered one half-step lower than the expected pitches. The student must listen carefully because the note will still tend to be sharp, even with the lowered fingerings. The C-flat is unattainable with standard fingerings on a four-valve tuba.

Figure 10–12 shows the fingering patterns with the fourth valve.

Professional-quality tubas have options for a fifth or sixth valve. These valves vary in length but are usually built to equal a flat 2–3 combination or a flat 1. These valves are added to give the performer more choices of alternative fingerings in the low register. With the five-valve tuba, a low C-flat is playable.

Figure 10–12   Fingering Patterns with the Fourth Valve

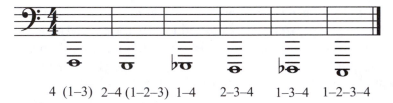

4 (1–3) 2–4 (1–2–3) 1–4   2–3–4   1–3–4   1–2–3–4

"False" Fingerings

Occasionally, music is written for the tuba lower than the fingering patterns allow. Use of false fingerings can make the notes sound. These notes will be very unstable and sound very thin. False fingerings should not be used unless absolutely necessary. It is strongly recommended that tubas be purchased with a fourth valve whenever possible. See Figure 10–13 for the false fingering pattern for the BB-flat tuba.

Figure 10–13   False-Fingering Pattern

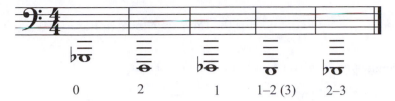

Warm-up and Practice Techniques

It is very important to have a comprehensive daily practice routine consisting of a warm-up, practice of fundamental techniques, and études and solo studies. The warm-up should consist of "flapping" or buzzing in the mouthpiece, simple scales, and lip slurs in a moderate range and volume.

The fundamental studies are often ignored by young tuba students. These studies should take from one-third to one-half of the practice time and should contain, but not be restricted, to the studies shown in Figure 10–14.

Figure 10–14   Fundamental Technique Studies
Perform the exercise in G, A-flat, B-flat, D, and C.

Play on all valve combinations.

Play in the keys of C, D, E-flat, A, G, and F.

Repeat exercise with following articulations:

Ranges

The recommended Register Guidelines for the tuba are shown in Figure 10–15.

Figure 10–15   Suggested Register Guidelines for the Tuba

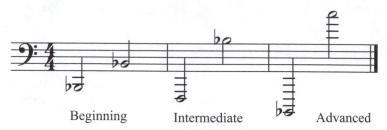

Beginning   Intermediate   Advanced

Specific Techniques for the Tuba

Vibrato

The vibrato is one of the most misused of the special techniques. Many tuba players use a vibrato "at will," without any thought to the role of the instrument.

The tuba is most commonly used as a harmonic instrument. If the tuba uses a vibrato while taking a harmonic role, there will be no stability in the foundation of the chord. Consequently, the intonation of the ensemble will suffer.

The only time that vibrato should be encouraged is in the playing of solo works, and then chiefly in the upper ranges. The notes on the tuba are very far apart, and in the lower registers a vibrato would have to be disturbingly large to be heard. The vibrato should be used as an embellishment to enhance the color of the sound.

The most natural sounding vibrato is the "diaphragm" vibrato. This type of vibrato is difficult to teach. If the student is going to use this vibrato, he or she must develop it naturally. Listening to tapes of solo performers will help a student to develop an ear for an appropriate vibrato.

The jaw vibrato is a very successful vibrato produced by moving the jaw as if saying "wah-wah." Care must be taken not to let the student close off the throat or raise the tongue during the production of this vibrato. The movement of the jaw is neither severe nor fast. If this type of vibrato is used improperly, tension may develop in the jaw and the sound and accuracy may suffer. If it is used correctly, it can help relax the jaw.

Lip Trill

The lip trill is an extension of the lip slur. The jaw will move much as it moves in the jaw vibrato. Many tuba players find that a slight movement of the tongue (a "yah" syllable) with the jaw will facilitate the trill. The throat should remain relaxed and open. The lip trill is used in the upper registers, where the harmonic partials are close together. It is important that the student have enough of a range to be able to comfortably play the notes in the trill. This is an advanced technique that should not be taught until the student has good flexibility.

Multiphonics

Multiphonics are becoming a common effect in contemporary literature. They are accomplished by playing a note through the instrument while simultaneously singing another note. It is easier to execute multiphonics if the student sings in a falsetto voice; however, most literature that has this effect is in a singing range that will require a full voice. This effect should not be approached until the student is performing the level of literature that requires it.

Transpositions

Transposition is very rare in the tuba literature. The only potential occurrence will be if the student is given a treble clef E-flat tuba part. This transposition is very easy: read the notes as if they are written in bass clef and add three flats to the key signature. Those tuba players who perform with F or E-flat tubas will generally not transpose; they will instead learn a new set of fingerings for the harmonic series of the instrument.

Choosing a Tuba and Other Equipment

Tubas

There are many different types of tubas, and they are designed to cover a variety of needs. Unlike most other brasses, the tuba varies greatly in size, the smallest being nearly the size of a euphonium. For school use, the BB-flat tuba is the only realistic choice. The BB-flat tuba is designed primarily as a tuba for the public schools. When choosing a tuba for schools, size is an important consideration. Some recommended models include the following:

Very Small Tubas

> Besson 797 (Three valves, piston)
> Yamaha YBB-103 (Three valves, piston)

Medium Tubas

> Conn 5J (Four valves, piston)
> Conn 12J (Three valves, piston)

Full-Sized Tubas

> Mirafone 1864U (Four valves, rotary)
> Besson 997 (Four valves, piston)
> Yamaha YBB-301 (Four valves, piston)
> Meinl-Weston Model 20 (Four valves, rotary)

The advanced student wanting to purchase an instrument has a more complex choice. CC tubas are used by the professional and the serious advanced student and are strongly recommended at this stage. These tubas are generally of a higher quality and are more responsive and delicate than BB-flat tubas.

CC tubas are not recommended for purchase by a school system. The student should contact a professional for recommendations and assistance in the purchase of an instrument.

Valves

Two types of valves are used on tubas: rotary and piston. Rotary valves need less maintenance than piston valves. However, there are more exterior moving parts on the rotary valve that can be damaged. These parts can generally be easily—but expensively—replaced.

There is little choice of valve type for beginners' instruments; most will have piston valves. Rotary-valve tubas should be used for the intermediate student. The choice of valve type for the advanced student should be whatever is offered on the tuba of his or her choice. If the student has a choice, the more advanced student should use piston valves; if properly maintained they are generally quicker and smother than rotary values.

Mouthpieces

The mouthpiece should fit comfortably under the nose and above the chin so that the embouchure makes a comfortable seal around the mouthpiece rim. For the young student, choose a mouthpiece that is not severe in any of its components. A medium-width rim, gently rounded with a moderate cup and backbore, will serve well. The Bach 18 is a good basic mouthpiece.

Recommended Mouthpieces

> Very small: Bach 32. This mouthpiece should not be used after the beginning of the intermediate phase unless the student is very small.
> Intermediate, average-sized transfer student, or advanced:
> Bach 18
> Conn 18
> Yamaha 18
> Conn-Helleberg 1205

The advanced student should choose a mouthpiece that gives a particular desired effect. At this stage the shape of the cup and rim, as well as the throat and backbore, influence the effect produced by the mouthpiece, and all these characteristics become a concern for the performer. Basic traits of the mouthpiece were discussed in Chapter 5, "Brass Instrument Equipment."

Mutes

The straight mute is the only mute used for the tuba in standard situations. Mutes of this type are commonly made of fiberboard, but the best are made of aluminum. The fiberboard mutes are far less prone to damage than the aluminum mutes and are therefore recommended for school use. The most popular brand of tuba mutes is the Stone Lined; they come in both fiber and spun aluminum. Practice mutes greatly change the way the instrument responds and are not recommended for the beginner or intermediate student.

Cleaning and Maintaining the Tuba

One of the biggest problems for tuba players in the schools is the condition of their equipment. Often students are required to play on instruments that are severely damaged. This damage is caused from a lack of cleaning and from improper storage. Tubas should be flushed out and cleaned at least twice per year, especially if they are used by several people. Flushing a tuba requires a large sink or tub.

Cleaning Procedure

1. Protect the tub and the instrument with a towel.
2. Remove all slides and piston valves. Rotary valves may not need removal; their care is discussed later in this chapter. Set aside the piston valves, taking care to keep the parts together and in order.
3. Soak the valves and slides in warm, soapy water. Do not use any abrasive cleansers on the valves. If the slides have excess sludge on them, a very mild cleanser may be used.
4. Use a snake to clean the insides of the slides, and use a soft cloth for the valves.
5. Soak the main body of the instrument in warm, soapy water prior to cleaning. This will help dissolve mineral deposits and oils that build up in the tuba.
6. After the tuba has soaked, use the snake and carefully ease it through the leadpipe and valve tubings. Be careful not to scratch or damage the rotary valves or the piston valve casings with the snake. Do not use an abrasive cleanser in the tuba; it may leave abrasive particles in the tubing and will eventually damage the valves. Do not depress the rotary valves—the snake will scratch the valve if contact is made.
7. Flush the tuba completely to remove the soap and film. A garden hose attached to the faucet is the best method. An adapter can be purchased at a hardware store.

Caution must be exercised if the tuba should need to be moved or lifted when it is full of water. The instrument will be very heavy, and severe damage will result if it is dropped.

Reassembly

After cleaning, dry everything, relubricate slides and valves, and reassemble. Use a medium-soft or soft anhydrous lanolin-based slide grease.

Recommended Brands of Slide Grease

> Yamaha
> Burt Herrick
> Holton

Put a small amount on each tube of the slide and work the grease with the fingers. Carefully align the slide with the tubes and gently push in the slides. Depress the valves if they are in place to release any pressure. Wipe off any excess grease.

When replacing the valves, it is important not to touch the valve. There are oils and acids on the skin that can damage the valve over time. Make sure the valve is rinsed completely. Use of a clean, soft cloth during rinsing will help remove any film or particles.

Lubricate the valve by placing several drops of valve oil around it. Carefully align the valve guide with the groove in the valve casing and replace the valve. Overtightening the valve cap can strip the threads or "freeze" the cap in place. Wipe off any excess oil.

Buff the instrument's exterior with a clean, soft cloth. Do not use cleaners or polishes on lacquered finishes. For silver finishes use a gentle cleaner or polish that will not remove any metal.

Maintenance

Preventive maintenance is the best way to keep the instrument healthy. Most exterior damage comes from improper storage. The tuba should be kept in a locker or similar place. Should there be no appropriate place, the instrument should be kept in a hard case in a safe area of the room.

Do not leave a tuba standing on its bell. This will cause the bell to flare; also, the instrument is easily knocked over in this position. Lay the tuba flat with the valve section up. The valve cage is very fragile, and placing the tuba face down on the cage can cause damage to the valve casings. Use a hard case when transporting the instrument. Soft cases (or "gig bags") can be used, but offer almost no protection against dents.

Valves are often the most neglected part of the instrument. Consequently, they often have the most problems. Piston valves must be oiled daily. An un-oiled valve will dry out, leaving deposits that will heavily wear the valve in a short time. To oil the valve, unscrew the cap and pull the valve out part way. Put a few drops of oil around the valve and carefully replace it.

The piston valve must be cleaned regularly, at least every few weeks. Follow the steps outlined earlier in this section.

Rotary valves need less attention than pistons, but there are a few tasks that must be done regularly to ensure a long, healthy valve life. Most care of the rotary valve does not require removal of the valve. The removal of the rotary valve is fairly easy; however, it is too involved and technical to easily explain here. Should a valve need to be removed, it is a good idea to take the instrument to a professional repair shop for instructions on the removal and replacing of the valve.

The rotary valve's exterior needs to be oiled more regularly than the interior. Remove the back cover of the valve (see Chapter 7, "The Horn," for illustrations of the rotary valve). Using a light machine oil such as Singer sewing machine oil, place a drop on the back bushing and pull the valve slide out a few inches. Repeat this step with the front bushings. The bearing on the linkage at the valve will also need regular oiling. This should be done every other week.

The rotary valve should not be removed often. If a rotary valve is stuck as a result of neglect and not outward physical damage, soaking the instrument is the only safe way to unfreeze it. If soaking the instrument does not work, do not force the valve. Take the instrument to a repair shop.

Valves are aligned by use of cork or rubber spacers. Periodic checking of these spacers is required. Misaligned valves can contribute to problems in accuracy, sound production, and intonation. In piston valves the spacers are found on top of the valve, under the cap, and on the underside of the valve button. These spacers should be replaced about every six months. To replace them, unscrew the valve stem and button and slip the new spacer in place. Cork is recommended over felt for the spacer on top of the valve.

Rotary-valve bumpers are located on the top plate of the valve. The alignment can be checked by removing the back cover and aligning the notches on the back bushing. If the bumper is too large, a small sharp knife or razor blade may be used to shave the bumper. If the bumpers are worn, they need to be replaced.

There are two basic types of bumpers: cork and rubber. The rubber bumper is the preferred type. New bumpers of either cork or rubber may be purchased at a repair shop and will be sized to fit the instrument.

To change the bumpers, follow these steps:

1. Use needle-nosed pliers to pull the old bumper out.
2. Gently pinch the new bumper with the pliers until it can slide into place.
3. Check the alignment of the valve.

History of the Tuba

Until the end of the sixteenth century, an adequate bass wind instrument did not exist. In approximately 1590, a bass version of the cornetto was developed in France. The instrument had an odd, curved shape resembling a snake, resulting in the name *serpent*. This instrument was generally made of wood, hollowed in the center, and bound by leather. The serpent had six tone holes, and it was these finger holes that created the biggest problem for the instrument. For the instrument to be acoustically accurate, the holes needed to be farther apart than the hand could reach. The holes were placed as accurately as possible, but the serpent had intonation and accuracy problems that were never solved. The size of the holes was also reduced from the acoustically preferred size to the size a finger could cover. Even with all these problems, the serpent was highly praised. The serpent was little used outside of France until the eighteenth century when it became popular in German military bands.

The serpent was large (8 feet long) and uncomfortable to hold. As the military band increased in popularity during the latter part of the eighteenth century, a need arose to find a bass instrument that could be easily carried. About 1780, the serpent was redesigned into a bassoonlike form by a musician named Regibo. This instrument was further developed in England by J. Astor. By 1800 the "bass-horn" had emerged. The bass-horn appeared in two basic forms: the "Russian bassoon," made of two parallel wooden tubes joined at the bottom by a U-shaped butt; and the "English bass-horn," generally made of metal tubes in a V shape. Most of these instruments retained the six finger holes of the serpent, and some had an additional four or more keys. Because of its similar design to the serpent, the bass-horn had many of the same problems. The bass-horn did not make the serpent obsolete. The serpent enjoyed greater favor in the church, and the bass-horn was rarely used outside the military settings.

About 10 years after the bass-horn was developed, the ophicleide appeared. This instrument was made in various sizes and was actually part of the keyed bugle family. The clavitube was the keyed bugle; the quinticlave was the tenor of this family, keyed usually in F; and the ophicleide, or bass ophicleide, was the bass, keyed usually in C or B-flat. The ophicleide was fully conical and had a large bore compared with the cylindrical tubing of the bass-horn. The instrument had eleven keys, and the holes were sufficiently sized and spaced to be acoustically accurate. This instrument was vastly superior to the serpent or bass-horn. It replaced the bass-horn in the military bands and was used in orchestral repertoire through the middle of the nineteenth century. Even though it was the superior instrument, it did not fully replace the serpent or the bass-horn. All three of these instruments were in use until the appearance of the modern tuba.

The first bass tubas appeared in Germany in 1835, patented by Wilhelm Wieprecht and manufactured by J. C. Moritz. The tuba was keyed in F and had a smaller bore than our modern versions. The earliest tubas were presented in the shape of the ophicleide, but were soon redesigned into the shape used today. Approximately 40 years after its appearance, the tuba fully replaced the ophicleide and serpent as the preferred bass voice.

The tuba has undergone many changes during the course of its short history. It has had as many as six valves of various types, the bore size has varied greatly, the preferred key has fluctuated, and the shape and materials of the instrument have undergone constant experimentation. These changes continue today.

Graded Literature Lists

Method Books, Beginning

Beeler	*Method for BB♭ Tuba, Book 1*
Ceib	*The Ceib Method for Tuba*
Couse	*Learn to Play the Tuba*
Hovey	*Rubank Elementary Method*
Kinyon	*Basic Training Course for Tuba*
Ostling	*Tunes for Tuba Technic*
Weber	*Tuba Student*

Method Books, Intermediate

Brightmore	*25 Melodic Studies for Brass*
Endresen	*Supplementary Studies for E-flat/BB-flat Bass*
Gower	*Rubank Advanced Method*
Hudanoff	*A Rhythm a Day*

Little	*Embouchure Builder for BB♭ Bass*
Prescott	*Arban-Prescott First and Second Year*
Skornicka	*Rubank Intermediate Method*
Vasiliev	*24 Melodious Études for Tuba*

Method Books, Advanced

Arban	*Arban's Famous Method*
Blazhevich	*70 Studies for BB-flat Tuba, Vols. I and II*
Bordogni	*43 Bel Canto Studies for Tuba*
Crigoriev	*50 Études*
Jacobs	*Low Register Studies*
Jacobs	*Restructured Études, Vols. I to V*

Kopprasch	*60 Selected Studies*
Kuehn	*28 Advanced Studies for Tuba*
Ostrander	*Shifting Meter Studies*

Grade 1 Solo Literature

Bell	*Low Down Bass*
Bell	*The Tubaman*
Buchtel	*Adonis*
Buchtel	*Ajax*
Buchtel	*At the Ball*
Buchtel	*Attila*
Buchtel	*Gladiator*
Buchtel	*Golden Glow*
Buchtel	*Pied Piper*
Buchtel	*When the Saints Go Marching In*
Fote	*Tubadour*
Merle	*Quintero—The Farmer*
Monroe	*In the Garden*
Petrei	*Asleep in the Deep*
Schlemuller	*Cradle Song*
Schlemuller	*A Prayer*

Grade 2 Solo Literature

Bell	*Elephantine*
Bell	*Gavotte*
Bell	*Jig*
Bizet	*Toreador's Song*
Edelson	*Tuba Tango*
Handel	*Air from "Judas Maccabeus"*
Kinyon	*Breeze Easy Recital Pieces*
Lotzenhizer	*A Hornpipe*
Lotzenhizer	*Solitude*
Merle	*Demetrius*
Merle	*Mummers*
Miller	*Tuba Tantrum*
Morra	*Nocturnal Serenade*
Rubank	*Mulberry Street Tarantella*

Grade 3 Solo Literature

Beach	*Lamento*
Benson	*Arioso*
Brooks	*The Message*
Buchtel	*Apollo*
Buchtel	*Il Penseroso e l'Allegro*
Christensen	*Ballad for Tuba*

Corelli	*Prelude and Allegro* from *Sonata no. 10, op. 5*
Geib	*Caprice in B-flat Minor*
King	*The Octopus and the Mermaid*
Kreisler	*Rondo*
Phillips	*Eight Bel Canto Songs*
Presser	*Rondo*
Scarmolin	*Introduction and Dance*
Sear	*Sonatina*

Grade 4 Solo Literature

Barnhouse	*Barbarosa*
Bell	*Folk Song Medley*
Bilik	*Introduction and Dance*
Buchtel	*Introduction and Rondo*
Cohen	*Romance and Scherzo*
Frankiser	*Melodie Romanza*
Galloway	*Essay for Tuba*
Geib	*Cavatina*
Goode	*Tune for Tuba*
Handel	*Adagio and Allegro* from *Sonata no.7, op.1*
Harlow	*Old Home Down on the Farm*
Howe	*Three Tuba Solos*
McCurdy	*Blues Basso Profundo*
McCurdy	*Troje*
Voxman	*Concert and Contest Collection*

Grade 5 Solo Literature

Arnold	*Fantasy for Tuba*
Bach/Bell	*Air and Bourée*
Bencriscutto	*Concerto*
Capuzzi/Catelinet	*Andante and Rondo*
Beversdorf	*Sonata for Tuba and Piano*
Corwell	*New England Reveries*
Curnow	*Concertino*
Defaye	*Suite Marine*
Haddad	*Suite for Tuba*
Hartley	*Suite for Unaccompanied Tuba Sonatina*
Holmes	*Lento*
McFarland	*Sketches*
Sibbing	*Sonata*
Tcherepnin	*Andante*
Vaughan Williams /Wagner	*Six Studies in English Folk Songs*
Vivaldi/Morris	*Sonata in A Minor*

Grade 6 Solo Literature

Broughton	*Sonata (Concerto) for Tuba and Piano*
Corwell	*Aboriginal Voices*
Ewazen	*Sonata*
Gregson	*Concerto*
Hartley	*Sonata*
Hindemith	*Sonata*
Jacob	*Tuba Suite*
Kellaway	*Dance of the Ocean Breeze*
Koch	*Monologue no. 9*
Lebedev	*Concerto in One Movement*
Russell	*Suite Concertante for Tuba and Woodwind Quintet*
Stevens, J	*Triumph of the Demon Gods*
Stevens, H	*Sonatina*
Swann	*Two Moods*
Tomasi	*Être ou ne pas être*
Vaughan Williams	*Concerto*
Wilder	*Suite No. 1 (Effie)*

Selected Discography

Bobo, Roger
Bobissimo! The Best of Roger Bobo, Crystal, CD125, ASIN: B000003J2J
BoTuba, Crystal, C392
Brown, Velvet
Velvet!, Crystal Records, CD692, ASIN: B00000JQJG
Coley, Floyd
The Romantic Tuba, Crystal Records, CD120, ASIN: B000003J2G
Friends in Low Places, Albany Music Dist., #501, ASIN: B000069JJG
Hanks, Toby
Toby Hanks, Tuba, Crystal Records, CD395, ASIN: B00004SG4J
Morgan, *Kevin*
The Virtuoso Tuba, Asv Living Era, #2098, ASIN: B0000030YX
Nelson, Mark
New England Reveries, Crystal Records, CD691,

Aboriginal Voices, Good Vibrations-RJR Digital, CD9630,
Perantoni, Daniel
Daniel in the Lion's Den, Summit Records, DCD-163, ASIN: B0000038K0
Pilafian, Samuel
Perception, D'Note Classics, #1027, ASIN: B0000067VZ
Pokorny, Gene
Tuba Tracks, Summit Records, DCD-129, ASIN: B0000038J1
Orchestral Excerpts for Tuba, Summit Records, #142, ASIN: B0000038JE
Self, Jim
Changing Colors, Summit Records, DCD-132
Sheridan, Patrick
Lollipops, Summit Records, DCD-221, ASIN: B00000AFJN
Blazing Brass, Summit Records, DCD-1012, ASIN: B00005YFO1

Selected Bibliography

Anderson, P. *Brass Solo and Study Material Guide*, Evanston, Ill.: The Instrumentalist, n.d.
Bevan, Clifford. *The Tuba Family*, London: Faber & Faber, 1978.
Cummings, B. *The Contemporary Tuba*, New London: Whaling Music Publishers, n.d.
Frederiksen, B., and Arnold Jacobs: *Song and Wind*, Windsong Press Ltd., January 1997.
Griffiths, John R. *Low Brass Guide*, Hackensack, N.J.: Jerona Music Corp., 1980.

King, Robert. *Brass Players' Guide*, North Easton, MA: Robert King.
Little, Don. *Practical Hints on Playing the Tuba*, Melville, N.Y.: Belwin Mills, 1984.
Mason, J. *Tuba Handbook*, Toronto: Sonate Publications.
Morris, R. W. *Tuba Music Guide*, Evanston, Ill.: The Instrumentalist, 1973.
The Tuba Source Book, Indiana University Press, April 1996.

Phillips, H. Winkle. *Art of Tuba and Euphonium,* Warner Brothers / Summy-Birchard Publications, January 1992.

Rose, William. *Studio Class Manual for Tuba and Euphonium,* Houston, TX.: Lola Publications, 1980.

Stauffer, Donald W. *A Treatise on the Tuba,* Stauffer Press, March 1989.

Vernon, C. *A Singing Approach to the Trombone,* Atlanta: Atlanta Brass Society Press, 1985.

Fingering Chart, Tuba (Combinations for four-valve tubas)

Harmonic Series, BB-flat Tuba

8va basso

| 0 | 2 | 1 | 1–2 (3) | 2–3 | 1–3 | 1–2–3 |

Exercises

The following exercises are designed to meet the needs of college or university brass methods courses of varying lengths, schedules, and curricula. These exercises are very different from exercises written for the young beginner in that they progress rapidly and assume knowledge of notation. The exercises also differ in that **they progress down the harmonic series rather than in diatonic scale patterns**. This system was adopted to better teach the seven-position or seven-combination fingering system used on the brasses. These exercises are divided into four sets: A, B, C, and D and should be assigned based on the schedule that follows. The instructor should choose the appropriate "course design" in the left hand-column and use the exercises marked by an x in the exercise columns. The exercise schedule is based on a course that meets 2 hours per week.

Course Design	A Exercises	B Exercises	C Exercises	D Exercises
16 weeks 1 instrument	X	X	X	X
16 weeks, 2 instruments	X	X		
16 weeks, 4 instruments	X			
10 weeks, 1 instrument	X	X	X	

The following topic list is suggested for the instructor or student who wants to focus on particular aspects of brass playing:

Long Tone Studies
    1A, 4A, 10D, 11D, 14D, 21C, 29B, 41B, 44C, 49B
Lip Slur Studies
    7A, 7B, 7C, 7D, 22D, 27A, 29A, 27B, 29D, 38A, 39A, 39B, 39D, 40A, 47D, 53A
Fingering/Position Studies
    14B, 14C, 17B, 17C, 17D, 23A, 23C, 25C, 28B, 30B, 34A, 47C, 53B
Chromatic Studies
    8A, 8B, 8C, 9A, 12A, 15A, 16A, 16C, 17A, 17B, 18A, 18B, 18C, 18D, 19A, 19C, 19D, 20A, 21A, 28D, 31A, 31C, 32B, 33A, 34C, 34D, 47A, 52D
Interval Studies
    8D, 13D, 14A, 15D, 19B, 20B, 22B, 24C, 29C, 31D, 32A, 37B, 39C, 48D
Single Tongue Studies
    9C, 9D, 10A, 10B, 11B, 13A, 13C, 15B, 16B, 21D, 22C, 24B, 25B, 28C, 42A, 42B
Double Tongue Studies
    40D, 46D, 48B, 49C, 49D, 50C, 51C, 53D

Triple Tongue Studies
    38D, 50D, 51B, 52C, 53C
Legato and Slurring Studies
    23D, 25D, 33B, 35A, 36D, 42C, 44D, 48A, 50A, 51D
Mixed Articulation Studies
    34A, 34D, 35B, 35D, 36A, 36B, 37C, 43B, 44A, 44B, 45A,
    46A, 46B, 50B, 51A, 52A
Four-part settings
    55D, 57B, 57C, 57D, 58B, 58C, 58D

Exercise 1A

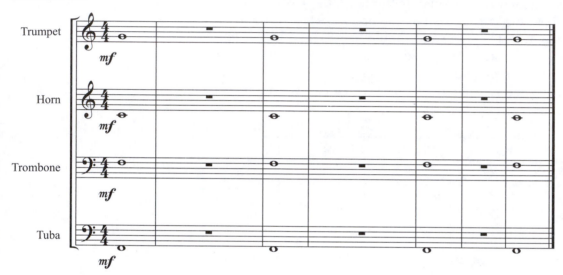

Exercise 2A

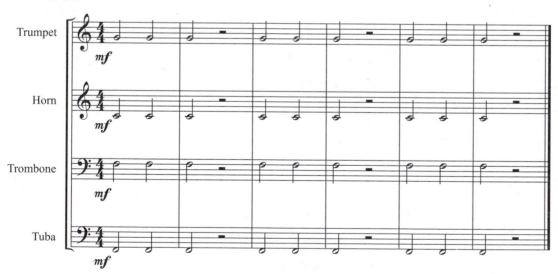

Exercise 3A

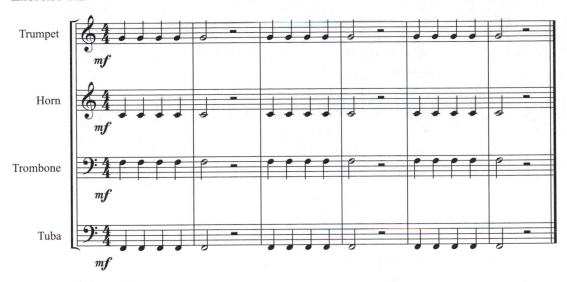

Exercise 4A

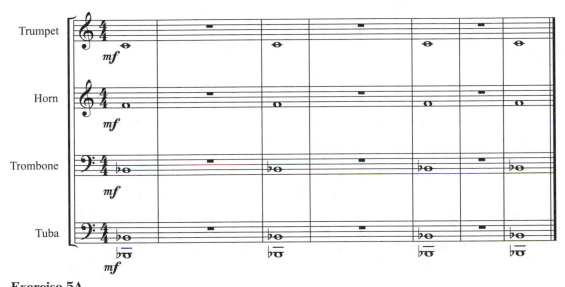

Exercise 5A

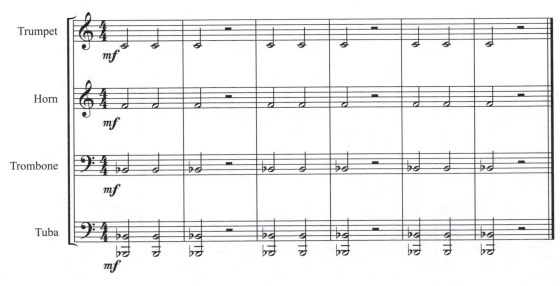

Exercise 6A

Exercise 7A

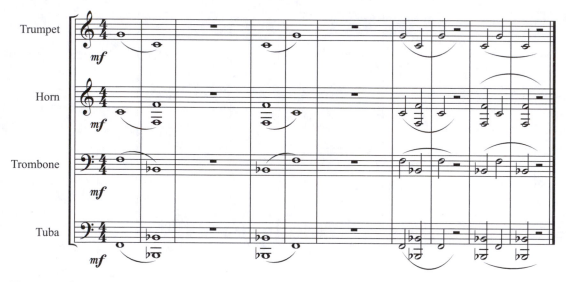

Exercise 7B

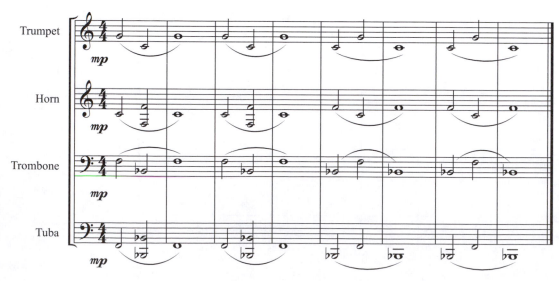

Exercise 7C

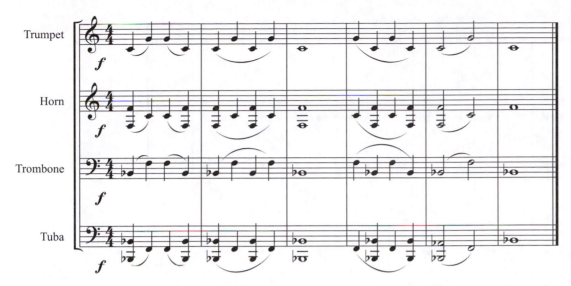

Exercise 7D

Exercise 8A

Exercise 8B

Exercise 8C

Exercise 8D

Exercise 9A

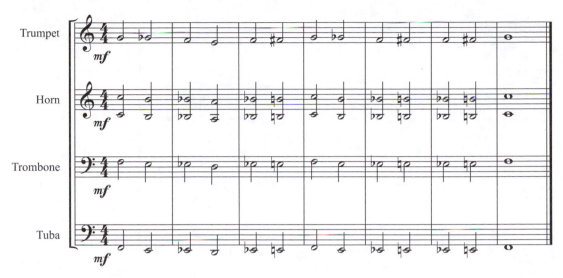

Exercise 9B

Exercise 9C

Exercise 9D

Exercise 10A

Exercise 10B

Exercise 10C

Exercise 10D

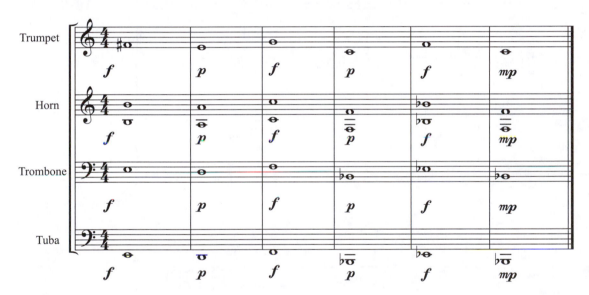

Exercise 11A

Exercise 11B

Exercise 11C

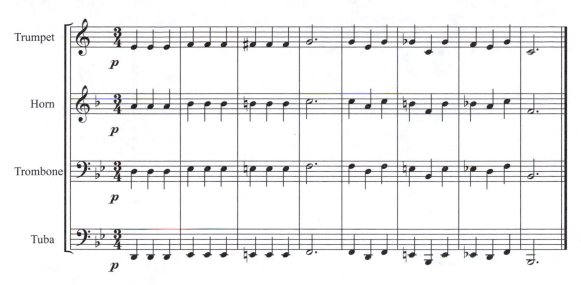

Exercise 11D

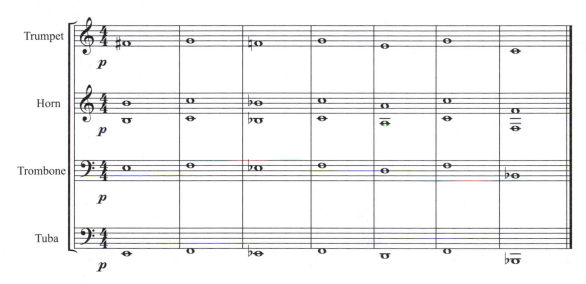

Exercise 12A

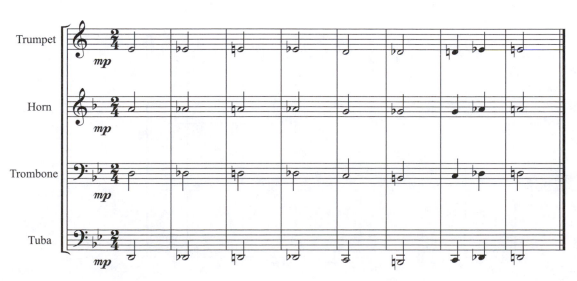

Exercise 12B, *Ode to Joy*, **Beethoven**

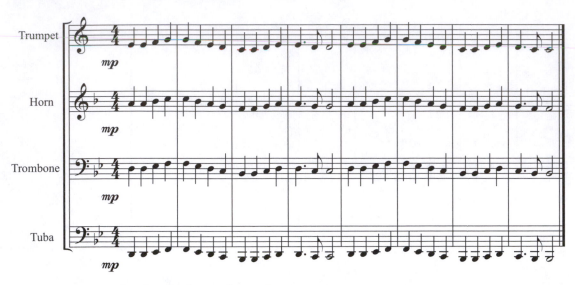

Exercise 12C, *Earle of Oxford March*, **Byrd**

Exercise 12D, *Sing We and Chant It*, **Morley**

Exercise 13A

Exercise 13B

Exercise 13C

Exercise 13D

Exercise 14A

Exercise 14B

Exercise 14C

Exercise 14D

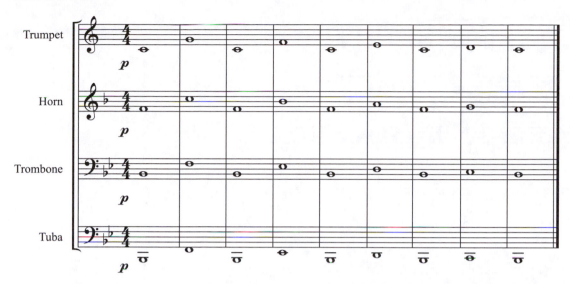

Exercise 15A

Exercise 15B

Exercise 15C

Exercise 15D

Exercise 16A

Exercise 16B

Exercise 16C

Exercise 16D, based on *Slavonic Dance no. 5*, Dvořák

Exercise 17A

Exercise 17B

Exercise 17C

Exercise 17D

Exercise 18A

Exercise 18B

Exercise 18C

Exercise 18D

Exercise 19A

Exercise 19B

Exercise 19C

Exercise 19D

Exercise 20A

Exercise 20B

Exercise 20C, *Alma Mater*, traditional

Exercise 20D

Exercise 21A

Exercise 21B

Exercise 21C

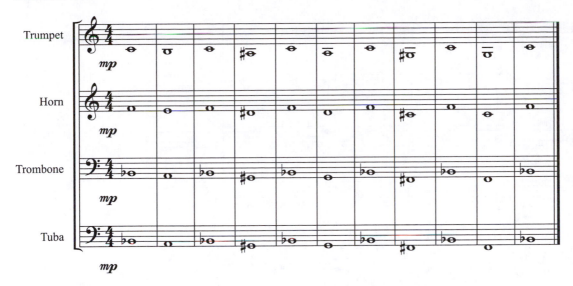

Exercise 21D

Exercise 22A

Exercise 22B

Exercise 22C

Exercise 22D

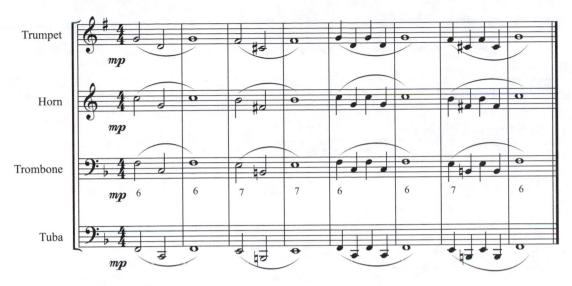

Exercise 23A

Exercise 23B

Exercise 23C

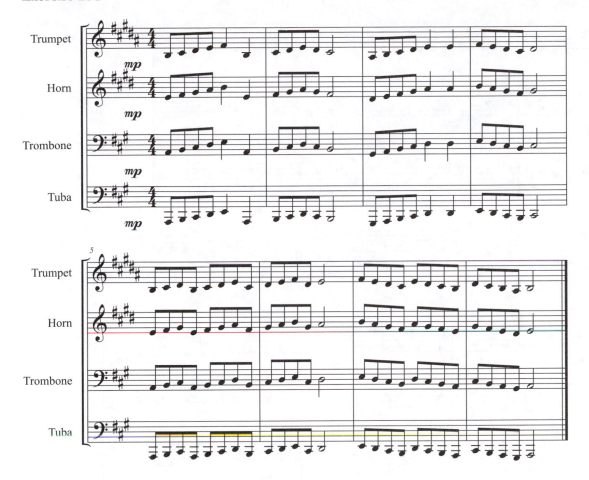

Exercise 23D

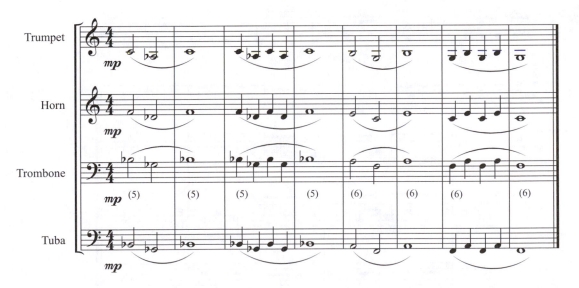

Exercise 24A

Exercise 24B

Exercise 24C

Exercise 24D

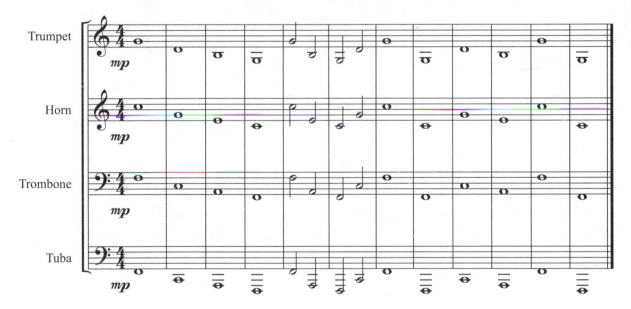

Exercise 25A

Exercise 25B

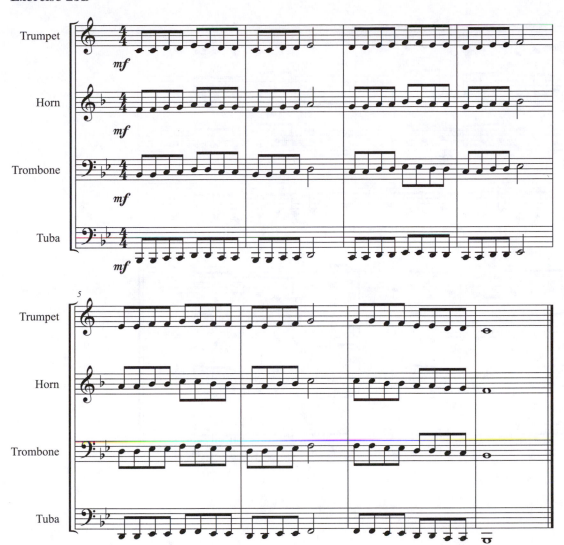

Exercise 25C

Exercise 25D

Exercise 26A

Exercise 26B, excerpt from *La Donna è Mobile*, Verdi

Exercise 26C, *New World Symphony*, Dvořák

Exercise 26D, *German Requiem*, Brahms

Exercise 27A

Exercise 27B

Exercise 27C

Exercise 27D

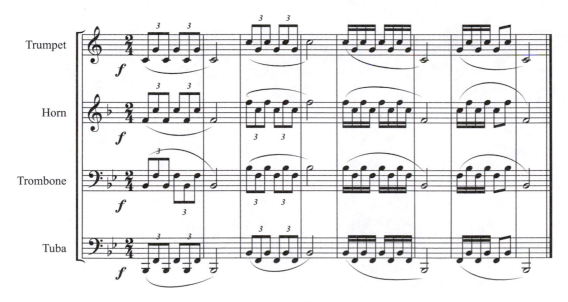

Exercise 28A

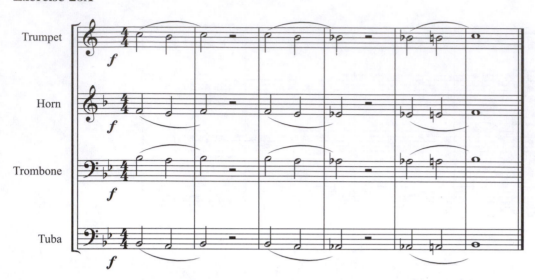

Exercise 28B

Exercise 28C

Exercise 28D

Exercise 29A

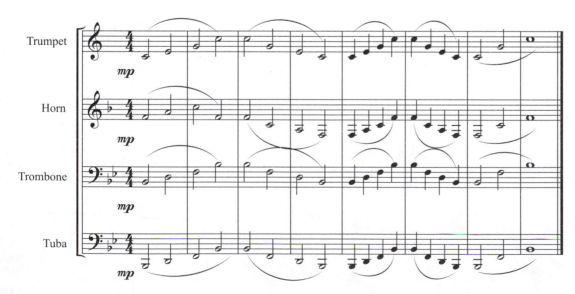

Exercise 29B

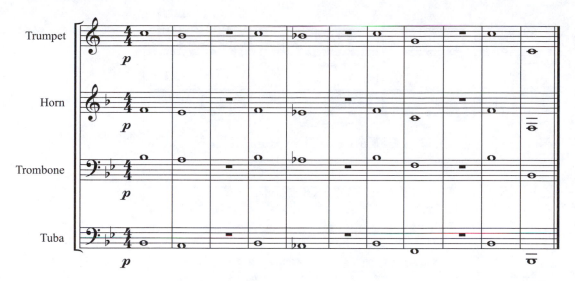

Exercise 29C

Exercise 29D

Exercise 30A

Exercise 30B

Exercise 30C, *España*, Chabrier

Exercise 30D, *Home on the Range*

Exercise 31A

Exercise 31B, *Country Gardens*, Grainger

Exercise 31C

Exercise 31D

Exercise 32A

Exercise 32B

Exercise 32C

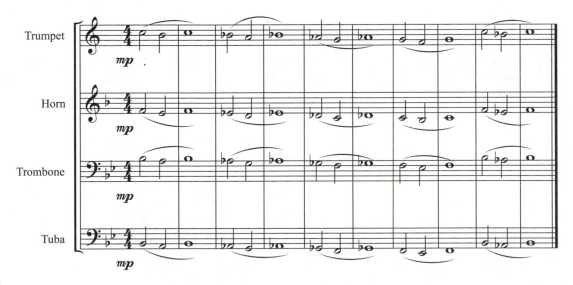

Exercise 32D, *"Surprise" Symphony*, Haydn

Exercise 33A

Exercise 33B

Exercise 33C *Buttercup*, **Sullivan**

Exercise 33D

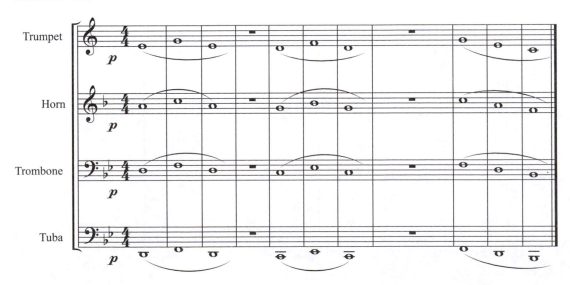

Exercise 34A

Exercise 34B, *Symphony no. 8*, **Beethoven**

Exercise 34C

Exercise 34D

Exercise 35A

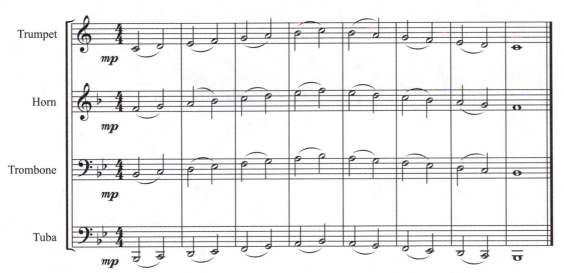

Exercise 35B

Exercise 35C, *Serenade*, **Bach**

Exercise 35D

Exercise 36A, *In a Cabin*

Exercise 36B

Exercise 36C

Exercise 36D

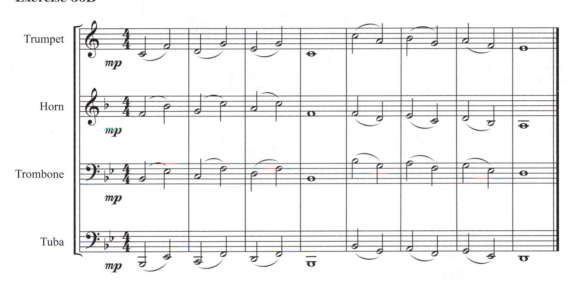

Exercise 37A

Exercise 37B

Exercise 37C

Exercise 37D *Symphony no. 7,* **Beethoven**

Exercise 38A

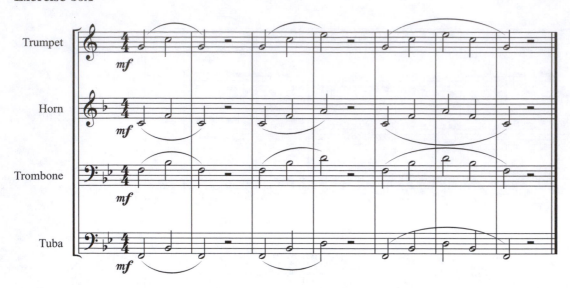

Exercise 38B

Exercise 38C *Symphony no. 6*, Tchaikovsky

Exercise 38D

Exercise 39A

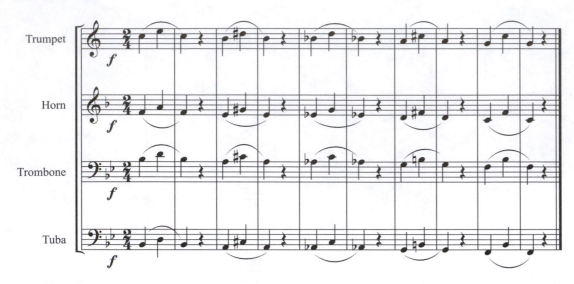

Exercise 39B

Exercise 39C

Exercise 39D, *Serenade*, **Schubert**

Exercise 40A

Exercise 40B, *Greensleeves*

Exercise 40C, *Symphony no. 1*, Brahms

Exercise 40D

Exercise 41A

Exercise 41B

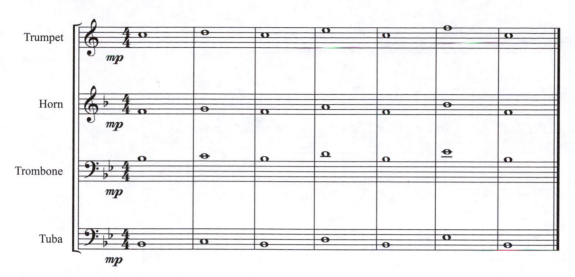

Exercise 41C, *Irish Tune*

Exercise 41D

Exercise 42A

Exercise 42B

Exercise 42C

Exercise 42D, *Symphony no. 6*, Beethoven

Exercise 43A, *Chester*

Exercise 43B

Exercise 43C, *If Thou Be Near*, Bach

Exercise 43D

Exercise 44A

Exercise 44B, *In the Hall of the Mountain King,* **Grieg**

Exercise 44C

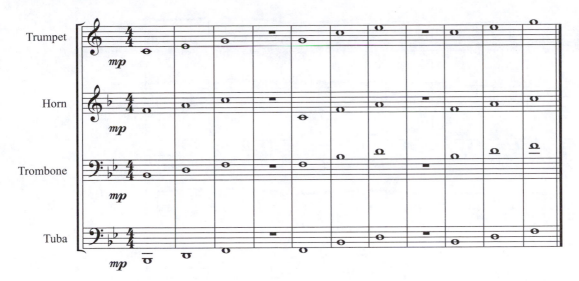

Exercise 44D

Exercise 45A

Exercise 45B

Exercise 45C

Exercise 45D, *Symphony no. 4*, Mendelssohn

Exercise 46A

Exercise 46B

Exercise 46C, *Toreador Song, Bizet*

Exercise 46D

Exercises

Exercise 47A

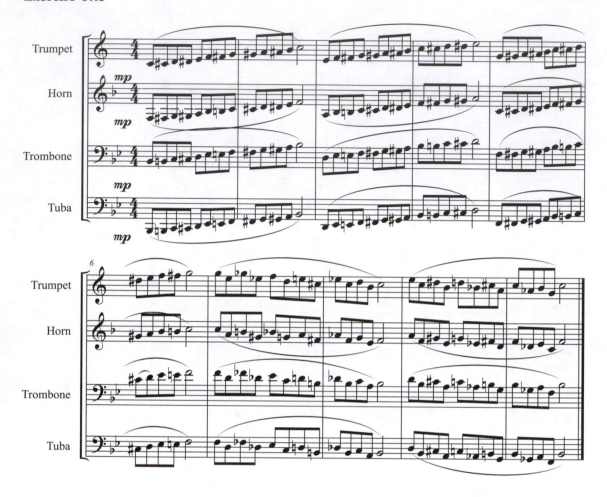

Exercise 47B, *Salvation Is Created,* **Tschesnokoff**

Exercise 47C

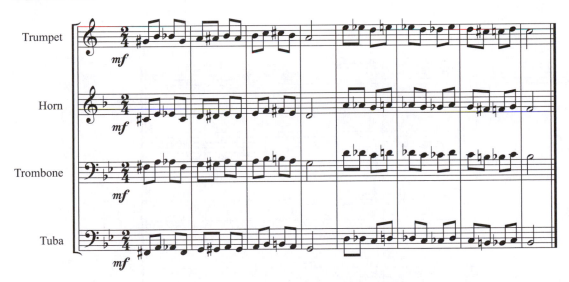

Exercise 47D

Exercise 48A

Exercise 48B

Exercise 48C, *Harkstow Grange*

Exercise 48D

Exercise 49A

Exercise 49B

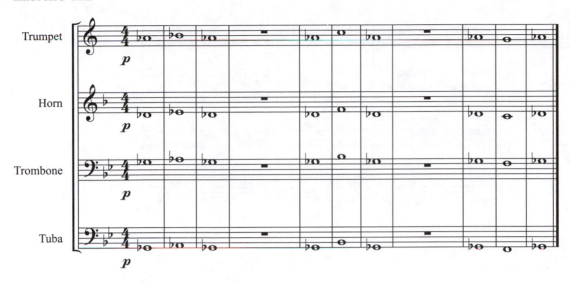

Exercise 49C, Double Tonguing

Exercise 49D, *La Bataille*, Susato

Exercise 50A

Exercise 50B

Exercise 50C, Double Tonguing

Exercise 50D, Triple Tonguing

Exercise 51A

Exercise 51B, Triple Tonguing

Exercise 51C, *Light Cavalry Overture,* **von Suppe**

Exercise 51D

Exercise 52A

Exercise 52B

Exercise 52C

Exercise 52D

Exercise 53A

Exercise 53B

Exercise 53C, Triple Tonguing

Exercise 53D, Double Tonguing

Exercise 54A, *Der Freischutz*, von Weber

Exercise 54B, *Petite Symphonie*, **Gounod**

Exercise 54C, *Can Can*, Offenbach

Exercise 54D, *Waggle Taggle Gypsy*, Traditional

Exercise 55A, *"Trout" Quintet,* **Schubert**

Exercise 55B, *Symphony no. 2*, Brahms

Exercise 55C, *William Tell Overture*, Rossini

Exercise 55D, *Farnabye's Conceit*

Exercise 56A, *Symphony no. 4*, Mendelssohn

Exercise 56B, *Leonore Overture no. 2,* **Beethoven**

Exercise 56C, *Academic Festival Overture,* **Brahms**

Exercise 56D, *Symphony no. 4,* **Tchaikovsky**

Exercise 57A, *The Irish Washerwoman*, Traditional

Exercise 57B, *Aria*, Gluck

Exercise 57C, *La Mourisque*, **Susato**

Exercise 57D, *Sonata Piano e Forte*, **Gabrieli**

Exercise 58A, *Simple Gifts*, **Traditional**

Exercise 58B, *Ave verum Corpus*, **Mozart**

Exercise 58C, *Variations on a Theme by Haydn,* **Brahms**

Exercise 58D, *Ayre*, Holborne

INDEX